TEACHERS HAVE RIGHTS, TOO

ABOUT THE AUTHORS

Leigh Stelzer is managing director of Capitol Research Associates, Inc. Joanna Banthin is assistant professor of management at the Stillman School of Business, Seton Hall University. Both Dr. Stelzer and Dr. Banthin were awarded Ph.D. degrees in political science by the University of Michigan.

TEACHERS HAVE RIGHTS, TOO

What Educators Should Know About School Law

Leigh Stelzer and Joanna Banthin

Social Science Education Consortium

ERIC Clearinghouse on Educational Management

ERIC Clearinghouse for Social Studies/
Social Science Education

Boulder, Colorado 1980

Library of Congress Card No.: 80-70053

Ordering Information

This publication is available from:

Social Science Education Consortium
855 Broadway
Boulder, Colorado 80302
(ISBN 0-89994-249-0)

ERIC Clearinghouse on Educational Management
University of Oregon
Eugene, Oregon 97403
(ISBN 0-86552-075-5)

Price: $7.95

This publication was prepared with funding from the National Institute of Education, U.S. Department of Education under contract nos. 400-78-0006 and 400-78-0007. The opinions expressed in this report do not necessarily reflect the positions or policies of NIE or the Department of Education.

To all of Kenneth's grandparents—the people who make it possible to get some work done.

CONTENTS

FOREWORD

In the course of our continuing work with teachers, we have become aware of their growing concern about how the law affects their professional and personal lives. Given the proliferation of governmental mandates about what, to whom, and how public education must be delivered and the increasingly active efforts of students and parents to define and claim their legal prerogatives, many teachers feel caught in the middle: while their responsibilities under the law are growing, their rights seem to be steadily eroding.

Much of these teachers' anxiety, we suspect, is due to lack of information about the extent and limits of their rights, as established by state laws and court decisions. In fact, even a hasty survey of judicial pronouncements and community attitudes over the years clearly reveals that teachers in the United States have more freedom today than ever before—certainly in their personal lives and probably in the classroom. Occasionally a teacher has abused this freedom; however, for every such teacher there probably are a hundred who have failed to exercise legitimate rights that they didn't know they had. To know and responsibly exercise their rights—at home, at work, and in the community—is an important obligation of teachers, as educators and as citizens.

The authors of this book have developed and presented programs on statutes, regulations, and court decisions that affect teachers and school administrators. Much of the data on which the book is based was collected during a four-year study, conducted by the American Bar Association with the support of the Ford Foundation, which was designed to analyze the relationship between law and curriculum change. Dr. Stelzer served as director of empirical research for this study, the results of which were summarized in 1979 in *Mandate for Change: The Impact of Law on Curriculum Innovation,* by Joel F. Henning et al. The Social Science Education Consortium and the ERIC Clearinghouse on Educational Management joined with the ABA's Special Committee on Youth Education for Citizenship in the publication of that volume.

We are pleased to have the opportunity to participate in publishing this book on the rights of teachers—a subject with important implications not only for teachers themselves but also for school building administrators, district officials, school board members, parents, students, and everyone who has an interest in public education. And that means all of us.

Irving Morrissett

Executive Director, Social Science
Education Consortium

Director, ERIC Clearinghouse for
Social Studies/Social Science Education

Philip K. Piele

Professor and Director
ERIC Clearinghouse
on Educational Management

PREFACE

This book is designed to address the law-related concerns of school teachers. School administrators, school board members, and school attorneys should also find the book informative and useful. Parents and students will find a goodly amount of relevant school law. However, the perspective is that of the classroom teacher. The issues are those which teachers regularly face in regard to their rights: tenure protection, RIF rights, student disciplinary options, negligence protection, freedom of speech, privacy.

This perspective has determined the content and emphasis of our analysis. The legal aspects of student expulsion are touched on only lightly, although teachers need to know that expulsion is a viable option and administrators and school board members need to learn the legal requirements. Similarly, we do not deal with students' First Amendment rights, school integration, or contract law.

There are perhaps two gaps in this book. First, although we describe teachers' rights to speak, assemble, and organize, we do not address the legal ramifications of unionization. Unionization—the rights of union members, collective bargaining, and collective action —is a technical and specialized field about which others have written. Furthermore, our discussions with teachers over the years have indicated that this is not an area of great concern to most of them.

Nor have we attempted to deal with some of the emerging issues in the legislative arena, among them teacher accountability and teacher competency. Most of the laws related to these areas are too new and untested to warrant analysis. For now, it must suffice to say that teachers have always been subject to evaluation by their supervisors. Tenure laws guarantee teachers due process, should evaluations lead to demotion or dismissal. Indeed, in at least one state (Washington) the courts have used a new statewide evaluation procedure to strengthen teachers' tenure protection. Constitutional guarantees protect teachers from invidious discrimination in the guise of evaluation.

Any book that tries to deal with the legal concerns of teachers in 50 different states necessarily suffers somewhat from overgeneralization. Every state has its own laws and individual peculiarities; what is true for one jurisdiction may not apply to another. Nevertheless, there are obvious consistencies in the education systems and education laws of the states. The Constitution and federal courts impose additional uniformities. We have tried to identify the established rules and the emerging rules and to convey a sense of the breadth and nature of the exceptions. Clearly, however, we do not pretend to offer the last word on the laws of any state or federal jurisdiction.

The law is not immutable; it changes all the time. It is changing in the courts, in the U.S. Congress, and in the state legislatures. If teachers don't like the legal decisions made by courts and legislatures, they can and should work to alter them. Teachers' rights are not gifts of a benevolent society. Teachers' rights are the hard-won results of numerous battles.

The research for this book has three antecedents: (1) our studies of school board politics and the administrative organization of schools, (2) our work with the New York State Assembly Committee on Education, and (3) our study of the influence of law on school teachers and administrators for the American Bar Association/Ford Foundation.

Over the years, we have benefited from the insights and assistance of many colleagues and friends. We owe basic intellectual debts to Tom Anton, Kent Jennings, and Donald Stokes. We also owe much to those who have shared their hands-on experiences with us; we particularly thank New York State Assemblyman Leonard Stavisky, New Jersey State Senator Matthew Feldman, and Robert Daggett, who showed us how education law is made.

Because this work grew out of the ABA/Ford study, we are indebted to colleagues and advisers at the Special Committee for Youth Education for Citizenship of the American Bar Association. We thank Joel Henning, Michael Sorgen, and Charles White. We thank Donald Sandberg, David Schimmel, and Isidore Starr.

We could not have written a book for public school teachers without the assistance of public school teachers. We thank the respondents to the ABA/Ford study who shared their concerns with us. We thank friends who have talked with us at length: Bob and Phylis Klein, Jason and Jeri Okin, Deborah Rosen, Bill and Paula Selzer, Diane Wessel, Bob and Ginny West. We thank members and officers of the Illinois Council of Social Studies and the Illinois Association for Supervision and Curriculum Development who gave us assistance and encouragement.

Several people have read and commented on drafts of this book. We thank Don Layton, Sheldon Miller, and Fred Rosenberg. And we thank our editor, Ann Williams.

Finally, we acknowledge the skill and persistence of Dolores Condon, who typed several drafts of this text.

Leigh Stelzer
Joanna Banthin

Teaneck, New Jersey
August 1980

INTRODUCTION

Teachers have come a long way in the last 50 years. Their professional image has changed. Ideas about what is proper behavior for a teacher have changed. And the law has changed.

In the past, the community expected teachers to be poor and meek. Dedication meant long hours for little pay. In many communities, teachers were held to the same expectations as were ministers' wives: no smoking, no drinking, no wearing flashy clothes or driving expensive cars; go to church, be a good family person. The cast-iron rule was: Thou Shalt Not Offend the Community. If teachers disagreed with the dominant social, political, or religious perspectives of the community, they kept it to themselves.

Just as teachers were neither seen nor heard outside the classroom, in the classroom the expectation was that they would be subservient to the community's social and political mores. If they stepped across the line, voiced opinions, or became controversial, teachers faced dismissal. And dismissal was arbitrary: there was no hearing, no appeal. After all, if a hearing was required, the teacher was obviously too controversial for the community.

Times have changed. Today's teachers have a new professional image. Laws and court decisions give teachers more protection from arbitrary community harassment. Strong organizations work to uphold the rights of individual teachers.

What rights do teachers have?

The area in which teachers have gained the most freedom is in the right to a private life outside the school. Most teachers now take for granted their right to a private life. Teachers can choose their friends, their organizational involvements, their community activities. Teachers can run their own lives, and they can even run for office. A teacher's personal affairs are considered private.

Of course, since teachers are entrusted with the care of minor children, there are some limits on their behavior. A teacher's life is private up to the point at which it interferes with the education of the children. Courts have said that school boards can dismiss teachers and administrators who commit crimes or admit to involvement in criminal activities. However, deviant sexual behavior is essentially a teacher's personal business as long as it remains private. Even if sexual exploits become publicly known, a teacher has some protection, including the right to a fair and impartial hearing. Furthermore, recent court decisions have held that before punishing a teacher a board of education must demonstrate that such activities will have a detrimental effect on students or the school.

How much of their own life styles can teachers bring into the school? There is some recognition that teachers can and perhaps should leave some aspects of their private lives at home. The courts recognize that a teacher is a citizen in a democracy, and that role models of democratic citizenship in the schools are desirable. However, teachers can bring their political convictions into the classroom. Generally, courts have ruled that the school should be a marketplace for the free expression of ideas. But the classroom is not a bully pulpit or a place to let out frustrations: there must be balance, equal time for competing viewpoints.

Good taste is a standard that teachers should uphold. Obscenity is not acceptable. Further, a teacher should not teach material that supervisors have expressly forbidden. But if a teacher believes that a taboo subject, person, or book belongs in the classroom, the court will listen to claims that the school board or administrators are inhibiting the free flow of ideas. The teacher may even win the case.

In many jurisdictions, teachers can go to work in whatever clothes they prefer. However, federal appeals courts have held that school authorities can reasonably request that employees dress in a way that is acceptable to the community. Nevertheless, if nonconforming dress reflects the teacher's personal, social, or political commitment it may be protected under the First Amendment. A teacher can probably wear a dashiki to express commitment to black liberation or a beard if doing so symbolizes commitment to the ideals of Abraham Lincoln. A teacher may wear an armband or a political button. However, freedom of expression may be limited if it can be shown that it disrupts the educational process.

Tenure provides an additional protective shield available to almost all teachers today. Tenure gives teachers the right to their jobs. Tenured teachers cannot be dismissed without due process of law or without cause; they are entitled to notice of charges and a fair hearing, with the opportunity to present a defense. The burden is on the school authorities to show that there are good and lawful reasons for dismissal.

"Live and let live" may be a maxim for happy living in the community, but the classroom is different. Teachers are responsible for their students. Their responsibilities are defined in statutes, court decisions, and local school regulations. Teachers must prevent students from harming themselves, other students, or school property. They must maintain order, and they must evaluate the academic progress of students.

Teachers may be charged with negligence if they are either too severe or too lenient. Teachers may not beat students into submission, but they are entitled to expect students to obey reasonable requests. They have the responsibility to protect their students and the right to defend themselves.

1.
TENURE

Tenure is the most familiar of teachers' rights. It is known to boards of education, administrators, teachers, teachers-to-be, parents, community groups, and students. It is an "essential safeguard to academic freedom," a "shield for incompetence," a "block to civil rights legislation," or a "barrier to change"—depending on who is describing it and what the problem is.

Tenure—sometimes called continuing appointment, permanent appointment, or continuing contract—gives teachers the right to the continued possession of their jobs. It is their primary guarantor of job security. Without tenure, a teacher's job is secure only for the specified duration of the contract. A teacher who has no contract serves entirely at the pleasure of the board of education.

The purpose of tenure is to protect teachers from arbitrary harassment by the public or the board of education. State legislatures have recognized that teaching can be a sensitive occupation. Teachers of high quality and integrity may come into conflict with ardent special-interest groups in the community. Tenure is a means for insulating the teacher from gross forms of political pressure and for ensuring a continuing supply of high-quality teachers.[1]

Legislatures in almost all states have granted teachers the protection of tenure.[2] Most of the last holdouts passed laws during the 1970s which granted tenure or increased the numbers of teachers covered by tenure. In 1980, only Texas and Wisconsin continued to deny tenure rights to large numbers of teachers.

Tenure is statutory, not contractual. Although states, not school districts, give tenure rights to teachers, such rights are limited to and valid only in the local school district in which a teacher is employed.

Tenure is job security. But how do teachers get job security? How long does it take to acquire it? What specific aspects of the job are secure: Teaching? Teaching a particular subject or subject area? Teaching at a certain grade level or range? Teaching in a particular school building?

Probationary Period

In all but a few of the tenure states, teachers must serve a period of probation before they are eligible for tenure rights. The length of the probation period varies. Mississippi, Vermont, and Washington have no probation period; first-year teachers have the same protection as their more-senior colleagues. Most states require two or three years' probation before granting tenure. Teachers in Indiana, Missouri, and Ohio must serve up to five years' probation.

Generally, teachers receive tenure automatically if their contracts are renewed beyond the probationary period set by statute. Since most states provide that a teacher's contract is automatically renewed unless notice to the contrary is given by a certain date (generally in April), school boards do not necessarily have to take positive action to grant tenure: teachers are awarded tenure when the school district fails to dismiss them by the end of the probation period. This "default system" has led to countless court conflicts about whether particular teachers are entitled to tenure.[3]

Tennessee is an exception to the default system. The Tennessee Supreme Court has ruled that tenure requires an *affirmative act* by the school board to reemploy the teacher.

Snell v. Brothers[4]

Billy Joe Snell was completing his third and final year of probation. Under Tennessee statute, if a school board does not intend to renew the contract of an untenured teacher it must notify the teacher by April 15. When the Rutherford County Board of Education failed to notify Snell by the statutory date that his contract had not been renewed, Snell claimed that he was entitled to tenure. The court, however, ruled that "a teacher does not acquire permanent tenure status by mere passage of time." The board's failure to notify Snell required only that his contract be renewed for one more year.

Limitations on Tenure Rights

What aspect of an educator's job is secure? Tenure gives an employee the right to *a position* with the school district; it does not entitle the employee to *a particular position.* Teachers are, however, entitled to positions comparable to those they held when they were granted tenure and for which they are qualified.[5]

Some states limit tenure to classroom teachers. The Arkansas Teacher Fair Dismissal Act defines a teacher as "any person, exclusive of the superintendent or assistant superintendent(s), employed in an Arkansas public school district who is required to hold a teaching certificate from the Arkansas Department of Education as a condition of employment."[6] Other states extend tenure to all certificated personnel. The Mississippi School Employment Procedures Law applies to "any teacher, principal, superintendent . . . and other professional personnel . . . required to have a valid certificate issued by the state department of education as a prerequisite of employment."[7]

The New Jersey law applies to "all teachers, principals, assistant principals, vice principals, superintendents, assistant superintendents, and all school nurses . . . and such other employees as are in a position which requires them to hold appropriate certificates issued by the board of examiners."[8] Additional New Jersey statutes extend the rights of tenure to school district secretaries and maintenance personnel.[9] The Louisiana law extends tenure to school bus drivers.[10]

Many states deny tenure to school administrators, particularly superintendents and principals. Kansas' teacher tenure law excludes "supervisors, principals, superintendent . . . or any person employed in an administrative capacity by any vocational-technical school. . . ."[11] The reasoning behind such exclusions is that school boards and top-level administrators ought to have full discretion in filling these positions. Often, however, the individuals who fill these positions are eligible for tenure as district employees. Although they have no tenure rights to their administrative positions, they do have rights to other jobs which they are qualified to fill within the district.

Tenure rights do not extend to a teacher's extra duties.[12] Assignment, reassignment, and withdrawal of extra duties is done at the complete discretion of the school board. Thus, teachers do not have tenure rights to positions as coaches, activity advisers, club sponsors, or monitors, regardless of whether such duties involve additional remuneration or whether they are specified in a teacher's contract.

Tenure is always systemwide; it is not limited to buildings or schools within a district.[13] However, tenure rights may be limited to certain subject areas, grades, or other full-time responsibilities—for example, counseling. Generally, states give teachers tenure as *teachers* and allow certification or experience to determine each teacher's competence to fill available openings.[14]

New York has a variety of tenure areas that limit the positions available to a tenured teacher.[15] Tenure is granted on the basis of grade levels (elementary, secondary) and certain specified subjects of an artistic or vocational nature (music, art, vocational education). Under the law, the commissioner of education and local school systems are permitted to specify additional tenure areas. The courts have recognized guidance, driver education, school-nurse teaching, and remedial reading as special subject tenure areas. The complexities and vagaries that surround tenure in New York are a source of constant litigation.[16]

Extent of Tenure Protection

Tenure laws protect teachers by enumerating the legal causes for dismissal of teachers with continuing appointments and specifying the procedures that govern the dismissal process. Generally, non-tenured teachers may be dismissed for reasons other than those enumerated in the tenure laws or for no reason at all. When non-tenured teachers are dismissed, they are usually not entitled to the procedural due process that is the right of tenured teachers.

Dismissal for Cause

State laws reflect an effort to balance teachers' need for protection from personally or politically motivated pressure against the desire of school authorities to maintain control. Typically, this balance is achieved by specifying a limited number of justifiable causes for dismissal. This list of causes usually includes various kinds of personal faults that a teacher may demonstrate and an open-ended reference to some unspecified "good" or "just" cause. In addition, many states specifically indicate that nothing in the tenure law limits a school board's power to revise its educational program or reduce its staff in response to financial constraints.

The tenure law of Connecticut is a succinct statement that contains all three of these elements:

> Beginning with and subsequent to the fourth year of continuous employment of a teacher by a board of education, the contract of employment of a teacher shall be renewed from year to year, except that it may be terminated at any time for one or more of the following reasons:
> • inefficiency or incompetence;
> • insubordination against reasonable rules of the board of education;
> • moral misconduct;
> • disability, as shown by competent medical evidence;
> • elimination of the position to which the teacher was appointed, if no other position exists to which he or she may be appointed if qualified; or
> • other due and sufficient cause.[17]

Illinois' tenure law contains the same basic elements, although its provisions are more complex and seemingly more nearly open ended. The law gives the Board of Education the power to

> dismiss a teacher for incompetency, cruelty, negligence, immorality, or other sufficient cause and to dismiss any teacher, whenever, in its opinion, he is not qualified to teach, or whenever, in its opinion, the interests of the schools require it, subject, however, to the provisions of Sections 24-10 to 24-15, inclusive. Temporary mental or physical incapacity to perform teaching duties, as found by a medical examination, is not a cause for dismissal. Marriage is not a cause for removal.[18]

A separate section of the Illinois Education Code deals with reduction in force:

> If a teacher in contractual continued service is removed or dismissed as a result of a decision of the board to decrease the number of teachers employed by the board or to discontinue some particular type of teaching service, written notice shall be given the teacher by registered mail at least 60 days before the end of the school term, together with a statement of honorable dismissal and the reason therefore, and in all such cases the board shall first remove or dismiss all teachers who have not entered upon contractual continued service before removing or dismissing any teacher who has entered

upon contractual continued service and who is legally qualified to hold a position currently held by a teacher who has
not entered upon contractual continued service.[19]

States vary somewhat in the personal faults that they list as
justifiable causes for dismissal. The faults most commonly cited are
immorality, incompetence, neglect of duty, inefficiency, insubordination, and incapacity, in addition to an open-ended category at the
end of the list. Courts usually interpret these open-ended clauses as
referring back to acts or events of the same type as those previously
enumerated.[20] However, school boards have argued (and some
courts have concurred) that such a clause should be interpreted as
meaning *any good cause.*

Not all tenure laws list specific causes; some are entirely open
ended.[21] Iowa's new continuing contract law cites "just cause" as
the only reason for discharge and contract termination. The state of
Washington's statute speaks primarily of "probable cause" and
"sufficient cause" for dismissal; the only specific causes mentioned
are lack of sufficient funds and loss of a levy election.

This lack of specificity has led the Washington courts to promulgate a new standard for determining whether causes for discharge are
sufficient.[22] They have read the dismissal law in combination with a
statute that requires school districts to systematically evaluate certificated personnel. An employee whose work is found to be unsatisfactory must be notified of his or her deficiencies and told how to
improve by February 1 of each year; the employee has until April 15
to demonstrate improvement. The court ruled that, given the new
law's requirement for annual evaluation of teachers, it follows that
"conduct, practices, and methods which can fairly be characterized
as *remedial teaching deficiencies* . . . cannot consititute 'sufficient
cause' for discharge unless [the law's] notice and probationary procedures are complied with."[23]

Property Rights

School board members and school administrators periodically
complain that tenure laws protect incompetent teachers. However,
there is no tenure law that does not incorporate incompetence as a
reasonable cause for dismissal. The real targets of such complaints
are the dismissal procedures designed to safeguard tenured teachers.

Many of the tenure dismissal procedures established by state legislatures, courts, and state departments of education are cumbersome. Furthermore, standards of fairness and proper procedure are constantly changing and evolving, and it is difficult for school authorities to keep up with the changes. Thus it has become common for school authorities to blame the courts when a dismissal is reversed on the basis that a school district failed to follow proper procedures. Some administrators use the tenure laws as an excuse for retaining incompetent teachers, even though the real problems may be inadequate supervision of personnel and insufficient documentation of grounds for dismissal.[24]

Although state tenure laws vary, federal court rulings have essentially standardized the dismissal procedures that school systems must follow. The U.S. Supreme Court has ruled that states are under no constitutional obligation to grant tenure to teachers. However, a state that does grant tenure gives teachers a constitutionally protected right to their jobs. A tenured job is considered a form of property; it cannot be taken away without due process of law.

The Fourteenth Amendment to the Constitution says that the state, including such creations of the state as school boards, cannot deprive a person of liberty or property without due process of law. For the courts, *property* is a concept that has gathered meaning from experience. Court decisions elucidate the attributes of property protected by due process. Thus, the Supreme Court has concluded:

> To have a property interest in a benefit, a person clearly must have more than an abstract need or desire for it. He must have more than a unilateral expectation of it. He must, instead, have a legitimate claim of entitlement to it. It is a purpose of the ancient institution of property to protect those claims upon which people rely in their daily lives, reliance that must not be arbitrarily undermined. It is a purpose of the constitutional right to a hearing to provide an opportunity for a person to vindicate those claims.[25]

Property is not limited to real estate or things; property interests encompass many types of benefits that a person may acquire. For example, in *Goldberg v. Kelly* the Supreme Court held that a person receiving welfare benefits under state standards defining eligibility is entitled to due process before the benefit can be revoked.[26] Similarly, in *Goss v. Lopez,* the court found that states which provide free public education to children cannot suspend or expel them from school without due process.[27]

How do we know whether a teacher has a legitimate claim of entitlement? One answer is that a claim is legitimate if it is objectively reasonable for an employee to believe that he or she can rely on continued employment.[28] A state tenure law that promises to continue a teacher's contract after a probationary period and to dismiss an employee only for cause supports a reasonable expectation of continued employment. The Supreme Court has ruled: "A written contract with an explicit tenure provision clearly is evidence of a formal understanding that supports a teacher's claim to entitlement unless sufficient 'cause' is shown."[29] By way of contrast, a contract with an explicit termination date which provides only for advance notification of dismissal, without specifying the need to show reason or cause, does not confer a property right.

Almost all states now provide explicit statutory schemes whereby teachers attain tenure. Contracts usually make it clear whether, and under what conditions, teachers have tenure. Yet the absence of explicit contractual provisions does not foreclose the possibility that a teacher has a property interest in reemployment: informal agreements or conduct may justify an expectation of continued employment. In *Perry v. Sindermann,* the Supreme Court ruled that a long-time instructor at a Texas college with no explicit tenure system might be able to show that he had a legitimate claim of entitlement to job tenure.

Due Process

Tenured teachers are entitled to procedural due process to demonstrate their continued claims to their jobs in the face of dismissal proceedings. Due process has a long legal tradition; Daniel Webster explained it as "the law which hears before it condemns, which proceeds upon inquiry and renders judgment only after trial." In the context of tenure dismissals, due process requires a set of procedures which ensure adequate notification of dismissal and a fair hearing.[30] Although the states differ on the exact details of the procedures, the essential elements are the same from state to state.

Adequate Notification

A tenured teacher has a right to adequate notification of dismissal. *Adequate notification* means both a detailed statement of charges and sufficient time to prepare a defense. The timing of notification and the sequence of procedures that must be followed by school authorities and teachers are spelled out in state laws.

A tenured teacher is entitled to a full statement of charges.[31] Courts have taken pains to distinguish between the highly general statutory causes for dismissal and the specific kinds of reasons or charges that are necessary to sustain a dismissal. The statement of charges must include specific allegations of wrongdoing, supported by information about time, place, and other circumstances.

Generally, if the charges are insufficiently specific to permit refutation, the teacher can ask for a bill of particulars in an attempt to force school authorities to provide a more-detailed statement of charges and evidence.[32] However, school authorities cannot introduce new charges, under the guise of greater detail, after a cut-off date specified by law.[33]

Some state statutes require a warning notice before school authorities can begin formal dismissal action against a teacher. In Illinois, before teachers can be dismissed for cause, they are entitled to a warning if the causes are "remedial,"—that is, removable or correctable.[34] Missouri law calls for a 30-day warning notice before a school board proceeds to terminate a teacher for incompetency, inefficiency, or insubordination.[35] California law entitles teachers to 90 days' notice in which to remedy teaching deficiencies.[36]

In many cases, courts have ruled that the failure of school authorities to follow prescribed procedures with regard to timing and notification nullifies a dismissal.[37] However, the courts do not view all elements of procedure as critical to ensuring due process; they have often been willing to accept substantial compliance with the law even when school authorities fail to meet precise requirements.[38]

Fair Dismissal Hearing

A fair hearing is the second requirement of due process. When teachers are dismissed, they must be informed of their right to a hearing. Generally, the teacher has a specified number of days in which to request a hearing; the hearing date is then set by mutual agreement. In Illinois, a school board is required to prepare automatically for a hearing unless the teacher requests in writing that no hearing be scheduled. In Wyoming, a school board must hold a hearing unless the teacher waives this right in writing.

A fair hearing requires several elements: The teacher is entitled to be represented by a lawyer and to present a defense which includes both giving evidence and cross-examining witnesses. Further, the teacher is entitled to an impartial decision based on the evidence presented at the hearing.[39]

The requirement for an "impartial" decision has generated the greatest amount of controversy. The standard procedure in dismissal hearings is for the school board to sit as both judge and jury. School board members are often called as witnesses against the teacher, and sometimes they even participate in the prosecution. It is difficult to see how a teacher can get an impartial hearing in these circumstances.

In the interest of fairness, some school boards have tried to limit their role to that of jury when they are permitted to do so by statute.[40] In this case, a board may allow an administrator to bring charges against the teacher and to prosecute the charges at the hearing, perhaps employing a lawyer to act as a disinterested judge. Whether a hearing can be "impartial" when a district administrative officer is assigned to prosecute a teacher is problematic. In any case, the fairness of such a procedure has been challenged in numerous state courts, with limited success. Citing instances of bias in the hearing procedures, some courts have reversed dismissals. For example, in *Monahan v. School District No. 9 Freemont County,* the Wyoming Supreme Court found that a tenured teacher did not receive a fair hearing when the school board designated its attorney to act as both presiding officer and prosecutor.[41] This dual role required the attorney to rule on objections to his own questions. Needless to say, he also ruled on his own objections.

For the most part, courts have viewed instances of bias as exceptions to otherwise acceptable systems. After the Pulaski Circuit Court ruled that the Kentucky dismissal law violated due process because the school board "is cast into and occupies the roles of employer, investigator, accuser, prosecutor, jury, and judge," the Kentucky Court of Appeals reversed the decision.[42] The appeals court noted that the law and the form of hearing mandated by prior decision "cloak a 'tenured teacher' adversely affected by board action with *additional and sufficient blankets of protection.*" In most such legal challenges, the availability of judicial review has been held to be an adequate and appropriate safeguard against gross violations of due process. The U.S. Supreme Court recently ruled, in *Hortonville Joint School No. 1 v. Hortonville Education Association,* that a school board's assumption of multiple roles in a dismissal hearing is not an inherent violation of due process.[43]

The Right to a Fair Hearing

The due-process hearing rights listed below have generally been upheld by the courts. Specific hearing rights may vary according to the state, the court, and the significance of the hearing. Any teacher requesting a hearing should seek in advance to ascertain his or her specific rights and to expand these rights if desirable.

- Timely and adequate notice of reasons and charges (in writing).
- Information about the names of witnesses and the nature of their testimony.
- Reasonable time to prepare for the hearing.
- Representation by counsel.
- Opportunity to be heard, to present arguments and evidence.
- Opportunity to subpoena witnesses.
- Opportunity to examine and cross-examine witnesses.
- Assurance that all testimony will be given under oath.
- Assurance that the hearing will be based exclusively on charges contained in the notice.
- An objective and impartial hearing officer or hearing tribunal which does not present or prosecute the case for dismissal.
- Assurance that all members of the hearing tribunal will be present to hear all evidence; absentees should not be able to participate in final decisions.
- Assurance that the decision will be based only on evidence presented at hearing.
- Transcript of the hearing (free or made available at cost).
- Statement of reasons for and evidence supporting the decision.
- A timely decision.

Hortonville v. Hortonville[44]

Teachers were dissatisfied with a new contract offered by the school board, and they went out on strike. After examining the options available, the board decided to fire all the striking teachers. At the original dismissal hearing, the board sat as judge and jury and determined that the dismissals were justified.

In court, the teachers argued that they had been denied an impartial hearing: How could the school board, which had provoked the strike and later chosen to dismiss the teachers for striking, impartially judge whether the strike was justified and the dismissals were appropriate? Although the teachers argued that there was an inherent conflict of interest in the board's dual role, they were unable to identify even one specific instance of bias in the board members' behavior toward the teachers.

The Supreme Court majority held that it had been proper for the board to try the teachers. First, board members had no direct financial stake in the decision. Second, mere familiarity with the facts was not sufficient to disqualify board members; indeed, even a board member who had taken a public position on an issue related to the dispute would not be disqualified, in the absence of evidence that he or she was not capable of judging a particular controversy fairly on the basis of its own merits. Third, the state and the voters vest school-board members with responsibility for employing and dismissing teachers: "Permitting the board to make the decision at issue here preserves its control over school district affairs, leaves the balance of power in labor relations where the state legislature struck it, and assures that the decision whether to dismiss the teacher will be made by the body responsible for the decision under state law."

A few states have removed the dismissal hearing from the jurisdiction of the school board.[45] Washington law calls for a hearing panel made up of three attorneys—one chosen by the teacher, one by the board, and the third by the other two attorneys. A new procedure in Illinois calls for the teacher and the board to select a hearing officer from a list of five candidates submitted by the state education department. Connecticut allows the school board to conduct the hearing but gives both the teacher and the board the option of appointing an impartial three-person panel to conduct the hearing.

Whether a decision is impartial depends not only on who makes the decision but also on what evidence supports the decision. A decision to discharge a teacher must be based both on the charges cited in the notice to the teacher and in the bill of particulars and on the evidence presented at the hearing. Furthermore, the hearing record must indicate the charges and the evidence accepted by the hearing officer as substantiating the charges. The courts have reversed a number of teacher dismissals on the basis of failure to meet these requirements.[46]

Interim Suspension

A school board may suspend a teacher in anticipation of a dismissal hearing if doing so is in the best interest of the school. However, the board must then quickly set a hearing date or reinstate the teacher. States differ in whether they pay suspended teachers: in Georgia, Michigan, Vermont, and some other states, suspended teachers are entitled to their salaries until hearings have been concluded.[47] Generally, suspended teachers who successfully challenge dismissal are entitled to back pay and, of course, reinstatement.

Nontenured Teachers

Teachers without tenure, whether they are on probation and/or teaching in districts without tenure laws, have property rights to their jobs for the terms of their contracts.[48] While under contract, they share the due process rights of tenured teachers and cannot be summarily dismissed. This protection is very limited, however, because most dismissals are effected by simply refusing to renew teachers' contracts. Lacking the right to continuing employment, teachers without tenure have no reasonable expectation of renewal and thus no property-right claim to due process.

Both legislatures and courts have been loath to limit the discretion of school authorities to decide on the retention of probationary teachers. The U.S. Supreme Court has ruled that nontenured teachers have no entitlement to continuing employment and, thus, no property-right claim when a contract is terminated.[49] A teacher whose contract contains an explicit termination date or lacks a provision that dismissal must be for cause does not have a property right to a position. As noted above, in *Perry v. Sindermann* the court left open the possibility that even in the absence of contractual provisions a teacher may be able to show reasonable expectation of continued employment. However, this possibility now seems remote,

given the large number of states which have adopted explicit statutory tenure systems. Thus, nontenured teachers whose contracts are
not renewed must rely primarily on the protection afforded by the
civil-rights and liberty-rights guarantees in the U.S. Constitution and
the limited procedural guarantees in state codes.

All teachers, of course, have civil rights, among them the rights
of speech, association, assembly, and petition.[50] However, the
knowledge that they cannot be fired for exercising these protected
rights is not particularly reassuring to probationary teachers, few of
whom are dismissed for such reasons. Furthermore, the Supreme
Court recently ruled, in *Mt. Healthy City School District v. Doyle,*
that a teacher must in the first instance demonstrate that protected
rights were involved in the dismissal and then prove that they were
the deciding factor.[51] The Doyle ruling means that it is irrelevant
whether some reasons for dismissal are unconstitutional as long as
there are additional, legitimate reasons.

A liberty interest is an interest in one's good name or reputation
as it might affect future employment opportunities or community
acceptance.[52] A dismissal that threatens a teacher's good name or
reputation threatens his or her liberty interest. In *Paul v. Davis,* a
majority of the Supreme Court held that there is no constitutional
right to a good reputation in the absence of loss of employment or
other tangible property or benefit: mere defamation does not invoke
Fourteenth Amendment due-process hearing rights. However, a
teacher who is defamed in a termination procedure would not face a
similar barrier—clearly, the loss of employment and the threat to
future employment eligibility would invoke constitutional protection.

Huntley v. Community School Board of Brooklyn[53]
*Claude Huntley had been the nontenured acting princi-
pal of New York City Intermediate School 33 for three years.
During that time, the school had been plagued by fires, hall-
way incidents, teacher complaints, and other problems. Prior
to dismissing Huntley, the school board made public a list of
charges. These charges included statements that Huntley
failed to demonstrate that quality of leadership necessary to
deal effectively with the educational program, that he was
responsible for the rapid deterioration of the school, that he
had not provided for the basic safety of the children and
staff, and that his lack of leadership had created a climate of
confusion and discontent.*
The U.S. Court of Appeals held that Huntley was

> *entitled to a fair hearing prior to the board's announcement of charges. The court said that the public statement of the charges made it unlikely that Huntley would ever have a chance to obtain another supervisory position—in the public schools or elsewhere. The charges went to the heart of Huntley's professional competence: in the words of the Supreme Court's Roth decision, the board had imposed a "stigma" that foreclosed his freedom to take advantage of other employment opportunities.*
>
> *The case was returned to the district court to determine the extent of (and appropriate relief for) the damage suffered by Huntley as a result of the board's failure to provide a timely due-process hearing.*

The Huntley decision shows that, although the courts may not help a teacher protect his job, they can help protect his good name so that he can get another job. Recognizing, however, that dismissal per se may make it harder to find another job, the courts have made it difficult to invoke liberty protection. In *Bishop v. Wood*, the U.S. Supreme Court ruled that if an employer is publicly silent about the reasons for dismissal—if the employer tells only the employee—the employee's liberty interest is not threatened. Further, dismissal does not threaten an employee's liberty interests if the reasons leak out afterward. Finally, whether the stated reasons are false or based on incorrect information is irrelevant: unpublished falsehoods are no more harmful to a person's reputation than unpublished truths. Thus, a teacher would seem to have no recourse should harmful information "leak" out to potential employers.[54]

Procedures for protecting civil rights and liberty interests are designed to shield teachers from gross violations of their constitutional freedoms; they seldom apply to the mundane considerations involved in the evaluation of probationary teachers, who must look to state statutes and court decisions for assurance of elementary fairness. Unfortunately, in the interest of maximizing the power of local school boards, many states give no protection to nontenured teachers. For example, Michigan requires only that teachers be given timely notice of unsatisfactory work, "whether based on good, bad or unstated reasons."[55] Tennessee does not even provide for giving notice to nontenured teachers, and the state courts decline to review nonrenewal decisions.[56]

Other states do try to protect nontenured teachers from arbitrary or unfair contract terminations.[57] Connecticut and Cali-

fornia require notice of reasons for dismissal as well as a hearing, if
the teacher requests one. Although New Jersey statutes are silent on
the rights of probationary teachers, the state supreme court has ruled
that in order to prevent the arbitrary abuse of power, a school board
must disclose reasons for dismissal (at the request of the teacher) and
must grant timely requests for informal dismissal hearings. Illinois
law requires that a school board give a second-year probationary
teacher "specific" reasons for dismissal, but no hearing is required.

On the face of it, a statement of reasons for dismissal may
appear to be of little value to a probationary teacher whose contract
has not been renewed. However, such a statement can be very
helpful. On the one hand, it tells the teacher what went wrong and
suggests ways of correcting deficiencies; on the other, it provides a
basis for assessing the legitimacy of the reasons cited and challenging
those that are not legitimate. As one judge noted in response to a
teacher's appeal, the school district's refusal to give reasons for
dismissal

> effectively forecloses her from attempting any self-improve-
> ment, from correcting any false rumors and explaining any
> false impressions, from exposing any retributive effort
> infringing on her academic freedom, and from minimizing or
> otherwise overcoming the reason in her discussions with a
> potential future employer.[58]

The potential risk involved in citing reaons for dismissal has not
been missed by school attorneys: publicly stating such reasons may
jeopardize the liberty interests of a teacher or may reveal that one or
more of the reasons are unconstitutional. Since a teacher may use a
school board's statement of reasons for dismissal to buttress civil
and liberty rights claims, district officials are often urged to keep
their decisions—and the reasons for those decisions—secret, insofar
as the law permits.[59]

Nontenured teachers should not take much encouragement
from requirements that reasons for dismissal must be provided.
Generally, the courts will accept a school board's reasons at face
value; any good reason is acceptable.[60] Reasons, the courts say, are
subjective—a matter of opinion, evaluation, and judgment. Therefore, a teacher cannot really challenge the *truthfulness* of reasons.
Finally, the U.S. Supreme Court's recent Mt. Healthy and Bishop
decisions severely narrowed opportunities to challenge reasons for
dismissal on the grounds of denial of civil and liberty rights.

Tenure gives teachers job security by providing for procedures that ensure fair dismissal. Teaching is a sensitive occupation. Teachers ought not be dismissed for partisan political reasons, nor for reasons that are arbitrary or capricious. Tenure guarantees a teacher due process in termination procedures and helps ensure that dismissal will be for just and demonstrable causes.

Notes to Chapter 1

1. A number of courts have commented on the purpose and goals of tenure; see, for example, *Redman v. Department of Education,* 519 P. 2d 760, 766 (Supreme Ct. of Aka., 1974): The purpose of tenure is "to give job security to experienced teachers and to ensure that they will not be discharged for inadequate reasons"; *Alabama State Teachers Association v. Lowndes County Board,* 289 F. Supp. 300, 303 (M.D. Ala., 1968): "There is a two-fold legislative purpose behind tenure laws and the tenure system: first, the laws and system give teachers security in their positions and guarantee the freedom to teach by protecting them from removal on unfounded charges or for political reasons; second, the system benefits the public generally by assuring a more competent and efficient teaching force"; *Rockwell v. Board,* 227 N.W. 2d 736, 737 (Supreme Ct. of Mich., 1975): "Goals sought to be achieved by Teachers' Tenure Act are: maintenance of adequate and competent teaching staff, freedom from political and personal arbitrary interference; promotion of good order and welfare of state and of school system by preventing removal of capable and experienced teachers at personal whims of changing office holders; to protect and improve state education by retaining teachers who are qualified and capable and who have demonstrated their fitness; and to prevent dismissal of such teachers without just cause"; *Ricca v. Board,* 418 N.Y.S. 2d 345, 348 (Ct. of App., 1979): "The tenure system is not an arbitrary mechanism. . . . Rather it is a legislative expression of a firm public policy determination that the interests of the public in the education of our youth can best be served by a system designed to foster academic freedom in our schools and to protect competent teachers from the abuses they might be subjected to if they could be dismissed at the whim of their supervisors."

2. According to Daniel and Richard Gatti, authors of *The Teacher and the Law,* (West Nyack, N.Y.: Packer Publishing Co., 1972, p. 130), in 1971 five states did not provide tenure to teachers: Mississippi, North Carolina, South Carolina, Utah, and Vermont. Another five states granted tenure only in specified urban locations: Georgia (Dekalb, Fulton, and Richmond counties), Kansas (cities with populations of more than 120,000), Nebraska (Lincoln and Omaha), Oregon (districts with more than 4,500 students), and Wisconsin (Milwaukee city and county).

In 1972 the National Education Association reported *(Teacher Tenure and Contracts,* p. 7) the same information for these states with one exception: North Carolina was listed among the states that authorized teacher tenure. Since the publication of these reports, it appears that all the states named except Wisconsin have adopted statewide tenure. See: *Georgia Code Annotated, Ch. 32-21C (1976); Kansas Statutes Annotated,* Sec. 72-5436 through 72-5439 (Cum. Supp. 1978); *Mississippi Code* of 1972, Sec. 37-9-101 through 37-9-113 (Cum. Supp. 1979); *McDonald v. Mims,* 577 F. 2d 951, (5th Cir., 1978); *Revised Statutes of Nebraska* (1943, Sec. 79-1254 through 79-1260, 1976); *General Statutes of North Carolina,* Sec. 115-142 (Supp., 1979); *Oregon Revised Statutes,* Sec. 342.825 (Replacement Part, 1973) and Sec. 342.805 through 342.9-0 (Replacement Part, 1977); *Code of Laws of South Carolina,* Sec. 59-25-430, 440 (Cum. Supp. 1979); *Utah Code Annotated,* Sec. 53-51-1, *Abbott v. Board of Education of Nebo,* 558 P. 2d 1307 (Supreme Ct. of Utah, 1976); *Vermont Statutes Annotated,* Sec. 1752 (Cum. Supp., 1979).

The Texas tenure law is permissive: school districts may choose whether they want to adopt tenure; see *Carl v. South San Antonio Ind. School Dist.,* 561 S.W. 2d 560 (Ct. of Civil App., Texas, 1978). The Wisconsin law limits tenure coverage to teachers in Milwaukee; see *Hortonville v. Hortonville,* 274 N.W 2d 697, 702, 703 (Supreme Ct. of Wis., 1979).

Although both the Gattis and the NEA reported that Arkansas provided tenure, as recently as 1977 a federal court held that Arkansas teachers did not have tenure. See *Clark v. Mann,* 562 F. 2d 1104 (8th Cir., 1977); *Cato v. Collins,* 539 F. 2d 656, 660 (8th Cir., 1976). In 1979 Arkansas adopted a new teacher tenure law, the Teacher Fair Dismissal Act; see *Arkansas Statutes,* Sec. 80-1264 (1979 Supp.).

It is not always easy to know whether a state has granted teachers the protection of tenure. In a recent decision, *Bishop v. Wood,* 426 U.S. 341 (1976), the U.S. Supreme Court held that even though on its face an ordinance may appear to confer tenure guarantees, the court is willing to accept contrary interpretations of state law by state courts and lower federal courts. This decision throws open to question whether South Carolina's law is a true tenure law. See *Adams v. District,* 241 S.E. 2d 897 (Supreme Ct. of S.C., 1978) for an interpretation of South Carolina's teacher dismissal law.

3.   *Ricca v. Board; Bonar v. Boston,* 341 N.E. 2d 864 (Supreme Ct. of Mass., 1976); *Plymouth v. State Board of Education,* 289 A. 2d 73 (Supreme Ct. of N.H., 1972); *Brunstrom v. Board,* 367 N.E. 2d 1065 (Supreme Ct. of Ill., 1979).

4.   *Snell v. Brothers,* 527 S.W. 2d 114 (Supreme Ct. of Tenn., 1975).

5.   *Berkner v. Board,* 373 So. 2d 55 (Fla. App., 1977); *McCullough v. Cashmere School District,* 551 P. 2d 1046, 1049 (Wash. App., 1976); *Goodwin v. District,* 226 N.W. 2d 166, 168 (Supreme Ct. of S.D., 1975); *Redman v. Department of Education,* at 766; *Sullivan v. Brown,* 544 F. 2d 279 (6th Cir., 1976); *Newby v. Board,* 368 N.E. 2d 1306 (Ill. App., 1977).

6.   *Ark. Stat.,* Sec. 80-12641.

7.   *Miss. Code,* Sec. 37-9-103.

8.   *New Jersey Statutes Annotated,* Title 18A, Sec. 28-5.

9.   Ibid., Title 18A, Sec. 17-2.

10. *Allen v. LaSalle Parish School Board,* 341 So. 2d 73 (La. App., 1977).

11. *Kan. Stat. Ann.,* 72-5436.

12. Ibid., 72-5437; *Kirk v. Miller,* 522 P. 2d 843 (Supreme Ct. of Wash., 1974); *Betebenner v. Board,* 84 N.E. 2d 569 (Ill. App., 1949); *Goodwin v. District.*

13. *Fedele v. Board,* 394 A. 2d 739 (Ct. of Common Pleas of Conn., 1977).

14. *Ward v. Nyquist,* 389 N.Y.S. 2d 638 (A.D., 1976) affirmed 400 N.Y.S. 2d 757 (Ct. of App., 1977); *Hagopian v. Board,* 372 N.E. 2d 990 (Ill. App., 1978); *Amos v. Union Free School District, No. 9* (364 N.Y.S. 2d 640 M.D., 1975).

15. *Baer v. Nyquist,* 357 N.Y.S. 2d 442 (Ct. of App., 1974); *Becker v. Board of Education,* 211 N.Y.S. 2d 193 (Ct. of App., 1961).

16. *Glowacki v. Ambach,* 385 N.Y.S. 2d 819 (A.D., 1976); *Chauvel v. Nyquist,* 389 N.Y.S. 2d 636 (A.D., 1976) affirmed 400 N.Y.S. 2d 753 (Ct. of App., 1977); *Ward v. Nyquist.*

17. *Connecticut General Statutes Annotated,* Sec. 10-151 (b)(5).

18. *Illinois Revised Statutes Annotated,* Ch. 122, Sec. 10-22.4 (Cum. Supp. 1979).

19. Ibid., Ch. 122, Sec. 24-12.

20. *Hartman v. Community College,* 270 N.W. 2d 822 (Supreme Ct. of Iowa, 1978); *Nutter v. School Committee of Lowell,* 359 N.E. 2d 962 (Mass. App., 1977); *Powell v. Board,* 550 P. 2d 1112 (Supreme Ct. of Wyo., 1976).

21. *Iowa Annotated Code,* Sec. 279.27; *Washington Revised Code Annotated,* Sec. 28A.58.450.

22. *Wojt v. Chimacum School District,* 516 P. 2d 1099 (Wash. App., 1973).

23. Ibid. at 1103.

24. A survey conducted by the American Association of School Administrators and published in *Critical Issues Report: Staff Dismissal: Problems and Solutions* (AASA, 1978, p. 42) listed ten reasons, suggested by legal experts and lawyers experienced in terminating teachers, why school districts lose dismissal cases: (1) they do not follow the law; (2) they do not adequately document their cases; (3) superintendents fail to adequately prepare administrative staff to understand the law; (4) the policy which the staff member supposedly violated did not exist in writing; (5) the district ignored the policy; (6) a district is not able to establish a case "even though the case is there"; (7) principals are not tough enough; (8) boards overreact and "go off half-cocked" without coolly analyzing the strength of their cases; (9) they get poor legal advice; and (10) they are overconfident about winning.

25. *Board of Regents v. Roth,* 408 U.S. 564, 571-572 (1972).

26. *Goldberg v. Kelly,* 397 U.S. 254 (1970).

27. *Goss v. Lopez,* 419 U.S. 565 (1975).

28. *Bishop v. Wood,* 426 U.S. 341, 353 (J. Brennan dissenting, 1976). See also the discussions in *Perry v. Sindermann,* 408 U.S. 593, 601 (1972) and *Stapp v. Avoyelles Parish School Board,* 545 F. 2d 527, 532 (5th Cir., 1977).

29. *Perry v. Sindermann* at 601.

30. The requirements of due process vary with the rights enjoyed by the individual and the potential degree of deprivation. See *Hostrop v. Board,* 471 F. 2d 488, (7th Cir., 1972); cert. denied, 411 U.S. 967 (1973). Also *Ferguson v. Thompson,* 430 F. 2d 852 (5th Cir., 1970); *Goldberg v. Kelly; Goss v. Lopez.*

31. *Powell v. Board; Wells v. Board,* 230 N.E. 2d 6 (Ill. App., 1967); *Hutchison v. Board,* 177 N.E. 2d 710 (Ill. App., 1974).

32. *Alexander v. District,* 248 N.W. 2d 335 (Supreme Ct. of Neb., 1977); *Mullally v. Board,* 164 N.W. 2d 742 (Mich. App., 1968); *Pearson v. Board,* 138 N.E. 2d 326, 329 (Ill. App., 1956).

33. *Lindgren v. Board,* 558 P. 2d 468 (Supreme Ct. of Mont. 1976). See also *Powell v. Board* at 1117.

34. *Ill. Rev. Stat. Ann.,* Ch. 122, Sec. 24-12; *Aulwurm v. Board,* 367 N.E. 2d (Supreme Ct. of Ill., 1977).

35. *Missouri Annotated Statutes* (Vernon's), Sec. 168.116; *Dameron v. Board,* 549 S.W. 2d 671 (Mo. App., 1977).

36. *California Education Code Annotated* (West's), Sec. 44938.

37. *Matthews v. Nyquist,* 412 N.Y.S. 501 (A.D., 1979); *Fatscher v. Board,* 367 A. 2d 1130 (Pa. Cmwlth, 1977); *Lindgren v. Board; Brunstrom v. Board; Flanders v. Waterloo Community School District,* 217 N.W. 2d 579 (Supreme Ct. of Iowa, 1974).

38. *Alexander v. District; Rost v. Horkey,* 422 F. Supp. 615 (D.C. Neb., 1976); *Glover v. Board,* 340 N.E. 2d 4 (Supreme Ct. of Ill., 1975); *Roy v. Board,* Decision of the Commissioner of Education of New Jersey (1976).

39. See note 30: "Not only is the teacher entitled to a hearing, but he is entitled to a fair hearing"; *Lusk v. District,* 155 N.E. 2d 650, 653 (Ill. App., 1959). See also *Monahan v. Board,* 486 P. 2d 235 (Supreme Ct. of Wyo., 1971) and *Miller v. Board,* 200 N.E. 2d 838 (Ill. App., 1964). For contrast see *Weissman v. Board,* 547 P. 2d 1267 (Supreme Ct. of Colo., 1976).

40. M.M. Jenkins et al., *Formal Dismissal Procedures* (Springfield, Ill.: Illinois Association of School Boards, 1977), p. 64.

41. *Monahan v. Board.* See also *Miller v. Board* (1964); *Glover v. Board,* 316 N.E. 2d 534, 538 (Ill. App., J. Craven dissenting, 1974); *Hortonville v. Hortonville,* 225 N.W. 658 (Supreme Ct. of Wis., 1975); reversed and remanded, 426 U.S. 482 (1976).

42. *Board of Education of Pulaski County v. Burkett,* 525 S.W. 2d 747 (Supreme Ct. of Ky., 1975); see also *Beattie v. Roberts,* 436 F. 2d 747 (1st Cir., 1971) and *Francisco v. Board,* 525 P. 2d 278 (Wash. App., 1974).

43. *Hortonville v. Hortonville* (1976).

44. *Hortonville v. Hortonville* (1976).

45. *Wash. Rev. Code Ann.* Sec. 28A.58.455; *Ill. Rev. Stat. Ann.* Ch. 122, Sec. 24-12; *Conn. Gen. Stat. Ann.* Sec. 10-151. See also *Ore. Rev. Stat.* Sec. 342.905.

46. *Kinsella v. Board,* 378 F. Supp. 54 (W.D.N.Y., 1974).

47. *Ga. Code Ann.,* Ch. 32-21C; *Michigan Consolidated Laws Annotated,* Sec. 38; *Vt. Stat. Ann.,* Sec. 1752(d). Illinois law does not mention teacher suspensions. A recent appeals court decision, *Craddock v. Board,* 391 N.E. 2d 1059 (Ill. App., 1979), dealt with a teacher who had been given a three-day suspension without pay for cursing a student. The 2:1 majority held that the teacher should have received the due-process rights prescribed for dismissals of tenured teachers before he was suspended.

48. *Perry v. Sindermann* at 576; *Wieman v. Updegraff,* 344 U.S. 183 (1952); *Connell v. Higginbotham,* 403 U.S. 207 (1971); *Merritt v. District,* 522 P. 2d 137 (Colo. App., 1974).

49. *Board of Regents v. Roth; Bishop v. Wood.*

50. *Perry v. Sindermann at 597;* see also *Pickering v. Board,* 391 U.S. 563 (1968) and *Shelton v. Tucker,* 364 U.S. 479 (1960).

51. *Mt. Healthy v. Doyle,* 429 U.S. 274 (1977).

52. *Board of Regents v. Roth; Patterson v. Ramsey,* 413 F. Supp. 523 (D. Md., 1976).

53. *Huntley v. Board of Brooklyn,* 543 2d 979 (2d Cir., 1976).

54. *Bishop v. Wood* at 348, 349. See *Hortonville v. Hortonville* (1979) at 702 for an alternate interpretation. In *Bowlin v. Thomas,* 548 S.W. 2d 515, 518 (1977), a Kentucky appeals court held that constitutionally protected interests are not impaired solely because reasons are false. In *Owen v. City of Independence,* _____ U.S. _____, 100 S.Ct. 1398 (1980), a majority of the Supreme Court adopted the position that a dismissed employee was entitled to a hearing if negative information became public even if the negative information was not released by the particular official responsible for the discharge nor contained in the discharge notice. It was sufficient that the charges were released by the city council and that their release was "contemporaneous and, in the eye of the public, connected with" the employee's discharge. A strong dissent by the four-man minority suggests that there will be additional refinements in the law.

55. *Lipka v. Brown City Community Schools,* 271 N.W. 2d 771 (Supreme Ct. of Mich., 1978).

56. *Shannon v. Board,* 286 S.W. 2d 571 (Supreme Ct. of Tenn., 1955).

57. *Calif. Educ. Code Ann.,* Sec. 13443; *Young v. Board,* 115 Cal. Rptr. 456 (App., 1974); *Conn. Gen. Stat. Ann.,* Sec. 10-151; *Donaldson v. Board,* 320 A. 2d 857 (Supreme Ct. of N.J., 1974). See also *Abbott v. Board.*

58. *Drown v. Portsmouth School District,* 435 F. 2d 1182 (1st Cir., 1970), cert. denied 402 U.S. 972 (1971).

59. Jenkins, *Formal Dismissal Procedures,* p. 54.

60. *Burns v. Fairfield School District,* 362 N.E. 2d 555 (Ill. App., 1977).

2.
REDUCTION IN FORCE (RIF)

RIF means "reduction in force." In the context of public education, "force" means teachers, counselors, supervisors, principals, and other certificated personnel.

RIF is a new experience in American education. After years of steady expansion, many school districts are simultaneously facing declining enrollments and rising costs for diminished services. This process of contraction has created a need for legal interpretation of existing statutes and contractual provisions. RIF has also motivated state legislators to write new laws—some designed to facilitate contraction and others intended to protect teachers.

RIF begins with a decision that a school district has too many teachers. Perhaps enrollments have declined. Perhaps a budget has been rejected. Perhaps enrollment patterns have changed. Perhaps the district has been reorganized. The state laws that regulate the hiring, firing, and job security of teachers generally provide for the elimination of teaching positions and the dismissal of excess teachers. The key phrase is "elimination of teaching positions." After a position is abolished, *then* a teacher is dismissed. "Elimination of position" is the reason for dismissal.

This explanation may sound straightforward, but the unsettled questions surrounding RIF are numerous: What requirements must be met for RIF to be declared? Who can be RIFed? What procedures must be followed? What safeguards must be recognized? How important is tenure? Seniority? Do RIFed personnel have reinstatement rights?

States differ in how specifically they regulate RIF. Typically, "decline in enrollment" or "elimination of position" is one of a list of possible valid reasons for teacher dismissal.

In some states, RIF seems to be covered under the umbrella of "dismissal for cause." In Connecticut, "elimination of the position to which the teacher was appointed, if no other position exists to which he or she may be appointed if qualified" is simply one of six causes for which a teacher may be dismissed.[1] It is listed in the same article as incompetence, insubordination, and moral misconduct.

By contrast, Illinois law distinguishes dismissals for cause from dismissals that result from a "decision of the board to decrease the number of teachers . . . or to discontinue some particular type of teaching service."[2] Illinois teachers who are RIFed are entitled to statements of honorable dismissal.

New Jersey law distinguishes RIF from other reasons for dismissal by delineating RIF causes and procedures in a separate article of the tenure law which affirms a school board's power to dismiss excess teachers. This article states clearly:

> Nothing in this title or any other law relating to tenure of service shall be held to limit the right of any board of education to reduce the number of teaching staff members employed in the district whenever, in the judgment of the board, it is advisable to abolish any such positions for reasons of economy or because of reduction in the number of pupils or of change in the administration or supervisory organization of the district or for other good cause upon compliance with the provisions of this article.[3]

Other state statutes are silent on RIF. For example, Massachusetts law simply provides that no tenured teacher shall be dismissed except for "inefficiency, incapacity, conduct unbecoming a teacher . . . insubordination, or other good cause."[4] Such language raises a question: Is RIF a "good cause"? In Massachusetts, the courts have answered, "Yes"; they have ruled that "good cause" is any reason that is not arbitrary, irrational, unreasonable, or irrelevant to the school board's task.[5] Since RIF is part of a board's planning function, it is a "good cause" for dismissal. However, courts in other states have not been so willing to interpret the vague term "other good cause" so broadly. In Oregon and Iowa, courts have ruled that "good cause" refers only to *personal faults of teachers* and not to conditions in the district.[6]

How Is RIF Justified?

By and large, RIF is a local school board decision. Only one state—California—specifies procedures for assessing preconditions for RIF. The California Education Code specifies the following formula for staff reductions: The percent of teachers RIFed can be no greater than the percentage decline in average daily attendance (ADA).[7]

Courts have been reluctant to become involved in defining preconditions for RIF; they tend to see making RIF decisions as administrative and educational functions of local boards. As the Pennsylvania Commonwealth Court declared, the determination of whether there has been a decline in enrollment "is an area in which school boards must exercise discretion, and board action will not be disturbed absent a showing that such discretion was abused or that action was arbitrary."[8]

Courts in the state of Washington have taken a different position. The Washington RIF statute allows teachers to appeal RIF decisions directly to the county superior court. The superior court must determine whether there is "sufficient cause" for the school board's decision, "which cause must be proven by a preponderance of the evidence." This statute, the court has said, mandates the review of RIF decisions in terms of evidence and testimony presented in court. The court's evaluation is independent of the conclusions reached by the school board.[9]

Who Gets RIFed?

Under RIF, a school district eliminates positions that are no longer needed. But how does a board decide which positions are unnecessary?

Various kinds of criteria can be invoked. In the elementary grades, enrollment figures indicate which grade-level groups will be smaller during following years. At the high school level, diminished demand for specific courses or programs may mark them—along with their instructors—for possible cutbacks. Some areas cannot be cut: all states require districts to offer a core curriculum and some specified services, such as nursing or testing. Such curriculum mandates place some restraints on cutback decisions. Thus, "frills" are identified—art, music, special-interest courses, remedial reading, counseling, enrichment programs—and courses that have small enrollments are singled out; for example, language classes, advanced math, advanced science. By this process, the "one position" or "two positions" or "ten positions" that are "no longer needed" are located.

Eliminating positions quickly boils down to dismissing teachers. At this point, district officials must decide the following questions: Who are (best) qualified to fill the remaining positions? Who gets to switch (bump) from a position that is eliminated to one that is retained? Who gets fired?

The most common bases for deciding which teachers are qualified to be retained for the positions remaining are *certification, evaluation, tenure,* and *seniority.* If all teachers are equal, there is a certain fairness in the traditional "last-hired, first-fired" policy in which untenured teachers go first and tenured teachers go in reverse order of seniority.

The critical problem here is that all teachers are *not* equal; they are different in terms of skills, training, and contribution to the school system. Furthermore, since neither declines in enrollment nor budgetary constraints always occur across the board, "qualifications" may be evaluated for particular subsets of teachers rather than for all teachers in a district.

Fedele v. Board of Education[10]

Joseph Fedele, a tenured music teacher in the Branford (Connecticut) Intermediate School, was dismissed when his position was eliminated. The school district had a declining enrollment and financial problems. The board saw a need for reduction in force, and chose to eliminate positions in non-academic areas.

In developing its RIF plan, the board recognized the three organizational levels of the district: elementary (K-4), intermediate (5-8), and high school (9-12). The board declared that "no tenured teacher will be terminated while nontenured teachers hold positions in the certification area within the organizational level being reduced." This policy prohibited "bumping" between levels.

Fedele challenged the policy. He said he was certified to teach music in grades 7-12 and was thus entitled to the position held by a nontenured music teacher in the high school. Fedele sued. He won. The court ruled that under Connecticut law, a tenured teacher is entitled to any position in the school system *for which he is qualified.*

Stets v. McKeesport[11]

Donald Stets, a tenured industrial-arts teacher in the McKeesport (Pennsylvania) Area School District, was dismissed after eight years of employment. The RIF began in the machine shop, when a decline in enrollment justified eliminating one of two positions.

The Pennsylvania School Code provides that teachers must be evaluated and ranked for purposes of determining who shall be suspended. Robert Watson was the lower-ranking teacher in the machine shop; however, Watson was also certified to teach industrial arts. Thus he could be added to the pool of industrial arts teachers—making that pool one person too large.

When the industrial-arts teachers were ranked, Watson was not the low man; Stets was. So Stets lost his job.

Stets sued the McKeesport School District. He lost. The court ruled that the board had acted properly and legally.

Hagopian v. Board of Education[12]

Robert Hagopian, a tenured elementary school teacher in the Tampico (Illinois) School District, was dismissed when his position was eliminated.

At the time of his dismissal, Hagopian held a teaching certificate known as Special K-14 for teaching and supervising physical education. He had taught courses in the social studies, spelling, science, and physical education at the elementary level.

After he received his dismissal notice, Hagopian requested that his credentials be reevaluated by the Illinois State Teacher Certification Board, and subsequently was issued a General Certificate for grades 6-12. He then asked the board to appoint him to one of the three positions held by nontenured teachers in the high school, since he was legally qualified to hold such a position although he had not taught in any of the three areas (band and chorus, industrial arts, and mathematics). The board refused to appoint him.

Hagopian sued the school district. He did not win. The

*court was not concerned with the fact that he had not taught
any of the subjects associated with the positions he sought.
The basis for the ruling was simply that on the day that the
board had to make its decision about Hagopian—at least 60
days before the end of the term, under Illinois law—he was*
not legally qualified *for the high school positions.*

Who Is Qualified to Stay?

Statutes and court decisions universally require that teachers
who are retained be "qualified" for the positions that remain. The
word—and thus the standard—is usually incorporated into state law.
Connecticut statutes make the dismissal of a tenured teacher contin-
gent on the absence of any other position for which he is *qualified.* [13]
Illinois statutes entitle tenured teachers to positions held by nontenured teachers for which they are *legally qualified.* [14] Pennsylvania
law entitles a suspended professional employee to reinstatement if
there is an opening that he or she is *properly certified to fill.* [15] The
California Education Code says that no permanent employee can be
terminated while a probationary or less-senior employee is retained
"to render a service for which said permanent employee is *certificated and competent to render.* [16] But what does "qualified" mean?
In practice, it usually means that the teacher must meet a basic
minimum standard; for example, certification.

Certification

The certification requirements spelled out in state statutes and
regulations can serve as a useful basis for assessing teachers' qualifications. However, some certification formulas are drawn so broadly
that they are of little practical use in ascertaining which teachers are
best prepared to fill remaining positions.

There are at least two types of teaching (as opposed to supervisory) certification: grade-level certification and subject-matter
certification. State certification schemes often integrate grade and
subject certifications at upper grade levels.

Grade-level certification is broad: it encompasses all the elementary grades or all the secondary grades, with sufficient overlap to
cover the junior high or intermediate grades. Subject-matter certification is necessarily narrower: it represents an attempt to keep up
with specialization in both learning and teaching.

States vary in the extent to which they certify narrower specialties and make such certification a condition of employment. Ohio's certification scheme is illustrative: the relevant statute identifies more than a dozen types of teaching certificates—among them kindergarten-primary (K-3), elementary (1-8), high school (valid for teaching subjects named in such certificates in grades 9-12), special (valid for teaching any specified subject in grades 1-12), and vocational—in addition to a variety of supervisory certificates.[17]

The Ohio statute is complemented by the state education department's elaboration of subject-matter fields.[18] Kindergarten and elementary certifications entitle teachers to teach all subjects within these grades. High school certificates, however, are divided into six fields: business, communications, family life, humanities, science, and social studies. The state department also issues certificates for such specialized high school teaching areas as visual arts, chemistry, and educational media. Teachers get these certificates by accumulating the appropriate course credits. Thus, the state certification pattern can seriously reduce the number of positions for which a teacher is "qualified."

In contrast, Illinois has a simple grade-level certification scheme: teachers are certified to teach elementary school (K-9) or high school (6-12).[19] In an effort to promote greater specialization in teacher preparation and assignments, the state commissioner of education has issued a policy statement recommending that teachers in secondary schools and departmentalized junior high schools have substantial subject-matter training.[20]

Two RIF cases have been fought over whether the commissioner's policy statement provides a legal basis for determining qualifications, and ensuing appellate court decisions have gone both ways. However, in January 1979, the Illinois Supreme Court held that the requirements were binding on school districts:

Lenard v. Board of Education[21]

Kenneth Lenard, a tenured teacher in the Fairfield School District, was RIFed from his position as a seventh-grade geography teacher. He claimed that his high school teaching certificate covering grades 6-12 entitled him to bump a nontenured sixth-grade mathematics teacher. The school board argued that, since some teachers left their homerooms to take math instruction from a second teacher, sixth-grade math was departmentalized. Lenard did not have the newly required 18 hours of math study that would legally qualify

> *him to teach a departmentalized math class.*
> *The Illinois Supreme Court ruled that the commis-*
> *sioner's policy had the force of law and was legally binding*
> *on the school district. Thus, certification and legal qualifi-*
> *cations were altered by the new policy. Lenard was not*
> *qualified for the position. His dismissal was lawful.*

This decision would have been a stunning blow to teachers if not for a subsequent change in the commissioner's policy, one which allows teachers five years to meet the necessary requirements. Unfortunately for Lenard, the policy was not changed until a few months after his dismissal.[22]

Seniority

When choices must be made from among "qualified" teachers, seniority is the most powerful factor in deciding who shall stay and who shall go. In some states (for example, Pennsylvania) where a ranking system is used, seniority is supposed to be considered "in the absence of substantial differences" in efficiency ratings.[23] However, seniority is one component of the efficiency ratings. In such states as New Jersey, the primacy of seniority is clear. The New Jersey Education Code reads: "Dismissals resulting from . . . reduction in force shall not be made by reason of residence, age, sex, marriage, race, religion, or political affiliation, but shall be made *on the basis of seniority. . . .*"[24]

The significance of seniority in New Jersey was highlighted in the Lascari case, which involved a teacher who had been a vice-principal for ten years before he was moved into another position. When his newer position was abolished, he bumped the incumbent vice-principal, despite the latter's five years' service on the job.[25]

Making dismissal decisions on the basis of seniority might seem to be a simple solution to RIF problems. However, there are some problems in using seniority as the major criterion. One problem is related to the way in which seniority is calculated: Does military service count? Are military years equivalent to teaching years, or should they be weighted? Does the inclusion of military years discriminate against women or others who were ineligible for service? These calculations differ from state to state. Second, there is the problem of identifying the most appropriate comparison group: Is seniority calculated in the teacher's subject? Department? School? School system? What happens if a teacher changes positions? Does seniority go along? The answers to these questions vary from state to state and with the traditions of individual school systems.

Generally, courts have accepted the idea that the relevant comparison group consists of those teachers who are qualified to teach in the remaining positions. Certification, specialization of tenure areas, and other qualifying factors may limit the size of this group. Pennsylvania courts have accepted departmental seniority as a basis for RIF.[26] New York courts have accepted tenure-area seniority as a basis for RIF dismissals of New York City guidance counselors.[27]

Seniority is not universally accepted as a basis for RIF decisions. In the state of Washington, teachers do not serve a probation period; thus, the courts have held that "every teacher under contract has certain employment rights which apply with equal force . . . without reference to length of service."[28] There is no statutory preference for employment on the basis of length of service. Washington courts have held that a school board must consider seniority only when it is among the board's previously adopted criteria for RIF.

Tenure

Tenure is one aspect of seniority. A tenured teacher may bump a nontenured teacher in a position the former is entitled to fill. However, a tenured teacher with little seniority is vulnerable under RIF.

What tenure does in the case of RIF, as it does in other kinds of dismissal proceedings, is provide for *notice* and a *hearing*. Because tenured teachers have a *property interest* in their jobs, they have a right to due process if any effort is made to take their jobs from them.[29] In a hearing, a school board must make its case for RIF and justify that particular dismissal. The hearing record can give an aggrieved teacher a basis for challenging the dismissal through administrative and judicial channels.

As noted earlier, in the discussion of the Fedele case (the teacher who challenged a board policy that teachers could not bump other teachers across organizational units of the district), there have been questions about where tenure resides. The courts have generally agreed that teachers receive tenure *in the districts in which they teach*.[30] Teachers may teach other subjects and move to other schools within the system if they are qualified to do so.

New York, as noted in Chapter 1, is an exception to the rule of systemwide tenure. There, the most common category for tenure is grade level—elementary or secondary.[31] School districts may also confer subject-matter tenure in physical education, art, vocational subjects, guidance counseling, driver education, school nurse/teacher, and remedial reading. This cutting up of the tenure pie severely limits bumping privileges. An individual may possess multiple qualifications and certifications, but can be tenured in only one area. Thus, teachers may bump only less-senior members of their own tenure areas in the event of RIF.

Glowacki v. Ambach[32]
Kathleen Glowacki taught Latin in the Roslyn (New York) School District. She was tenured as a secondary teacher. Her position was eliminated in a RIF. She applied for one of two openings in the guidance department. Her claim to a position in guidance was buttressed by the following evidence: She had filled a temporary vacancy in guidance for one semester and she had received provisional certification as a guidance counselor. The board claimed that guidance was a recognized separate tenure area; thus, Glowacki had no right to the vacancy. The court agreed.

The Right of Return

It seems only fair that teachers who have been RIFed should have priority claims to jobs that subsequently open up in a school system. However, fairness and legal rights are not always the same.

In some states, both tenured and nontenured teachers who have been RIFed have priority claims to jobs that open in the district. New Jersey law provides for the reinstatement of all staff on the basis of seniority and qualification.[33]

In other states—Illinois and Pennsylvania, for example—only teachers who had tenure when they were RIFed have claims on jobs.[34] Pennsylvania statutes require school districts to reinstate tenured employees in inverse order of their suspension; no new appointments may be made as long as properly certified suspended tenured teachers are available to fill the vacancies. Pennsylvania courts have made it clear that suspended teachers have priority claims, not only on their old positions but on any openings for which they are qualified.

RIFed tenured teachers in Illinois have reinstatement rights for one year following dismissal. They are entitled to reemployment if the school district *increases* the number of teachers in the district or *restores* discontinued positions.

There have been conflicts over the meaning of the word "increase" in the Illinois statute. In more than one district, after the staff was RIFed down to the number of teachers the district could support, additional teachers left voluntarily. Boards argued that they did not have to fill these vacancies with RIFed teachers because they were not increasing the *numbers* of staff members in their systems. The courts have not accepted this argument.[35] They have said that RIFed tenured teachers are entitled to priority in filling *any* opening.

Ironically, the right to "any" position may exclude teachers from their old positions. The California Supreme Court has ruled that, although terminated teachers have a right to appointment should their positions be reestablished, teachers who have been reassigned under RIF have no right to reinstatement to their old positions.[36]

Contracts

Will a contract provision that specifies RIF procedures protect teachers? In a word, maybe.

In anticipation of RIF, teachers and their organizations have tried to get RIF procedures defined in their contracts, and most contracts contain statements about formulas to be used in deciding who shall be retained. Such formulas may mention evaluation, seniority, service, and other factors that the teachers and board consider to be important.

The value of such a statement in a contract is necessarily limited. Hiring and firing are discretionary functions of a school board which generally cannot be delegated. Boards must make decisions; they cannot be committed to retaining positions which they find they need to eliminate. A New Jersey Supreme Court decision is instructive:

Board of Education v. Englewood Teachers Association[37]
For reasons of economy and efficiency, the Englewood (New Jersey) Board of Education decided to close a school, redistribute the tenured staff, and dismiss about 40 nontenured teachers. The teachers' association challenged the reasons for the dismissals. The court concluded that the determination not to renew the contract of a nontenured teacher was "a discretionary matter for the local board. . . . As a corollary, the statutory power to reduce personnel . . . cannot be the subject of negotiation or arbitration."

The Illinois Supreme Court used similar language in a case dealing with the dismissal of a probationary teacher.[38] The school authorities had dismissed the teacher at the end of his probationary period without following the evaluation procedures established by a collective bargaining agreement. Two lower courts held that the teacher had been dismissed improperly and ordered him reinstated with tenure. The Illinois Supreme Court, however, held that neither the powers conferred nor the rights granted by the tenure laws were restricted or expanded by the contract. The teacher was dismissed.

While the courts have been unsympathetic to contract provisions that restrict a board's power to hire and fire, they have required school authorities to comply with laws that introduce due-process fairness into the decision. Furthermore, contract provisions that introduce fairness into the procedure without limiting a board's power have been upheld by the courts. Thus, when a teacher was transferred without evaluation and was denied the hearing for which his contract provided, an Illinois appellate court upheld the teacher's right to these procedures.[39] Similarly, when a New York school board RIFed all of its nurse/teachers, the court held that it could enforce a contract provision that obligated the school board, "in the event of layoff . . . [to] make every effort to insure that separated personnel . . . be placed in other teaching situations."[40]

Teachers might benefit additionally from contract provisions that give them a role in planning the academic program. Decisions about course offerings and requirements very quickly become decisions on how many teachers, in what fields, will be needed.

Here we must distinguish between the law and common sense: curriculum is the responsibility of a school board and a board cannot legally negotiate away this power. As a Washington state court of appeals noted, "The determination of educational goals, programs, and curricula is a matter within the broad discretion of the school board . . . the law does not require the school board to consider the availability of teachers with specific qualifications in establishing the district goals or requirements. The efficient use of combinations of teaching skills into teaching assignment is within the broad discretionary powers of the school board."[41]

Though boards have the broad discretionary power to determine curricula, it seems reasonable to share this responsibility with professional educators. Furthermore, it seems reasonable for a contract to specify a method of curriculum planning which considers the skills and experience of the present faculty. Nothing precludes a board from adopting a RIF method that would maximize opportunities for the retention of personnel. The incorporation of such a goal in contracts and guidelines is reasonable and is consistent with the tenure rights of teachers. While the courts may accept this type of contract provision, it is unclear what limits they will be willing to enforce on school-board discretion in cases of conflict between teachers' organizations and boards of education.

Transfer

School authorities have the responsibility and the right to assign personnel to positions on the basis of what they believe will best achieve the goals of education. They have a great deal of discretion in assigning and transferring personnel. This discretion is limited, however, by teachers' certification, seniority, tenure, property rights, and civil rights.

Certification limits the discretion of school authorities because, normally, they cannot assign professional personnel to positions for which they are not certified.[42] Their freedom of action is most restricted in states that have a large number of gradations or categories in certification. Discretion is maximized in states with the broadest categories of certification and in states that allow temporary or provisional appointments pending certification.

Seniority places an additional limit on school-board discretion in states that recognize teachers' seniority rights. Teachers and administrators with greater seniority generally have the right to "bump," or assume the positions of, persons with less seniority. School authorities must recognize seniority rights when making transfers.

Tenure is an additional limiting factor. As we noted in Chapter 1, tenure entitles a person to *a* position with the school district, but not to any particular position. However, holding a particular position implies a right to a position that is essentially similar in pay, status, and responsibility. Thus school authorities are free to make lateral transfers that do not diminish the benefits conferred on the teacher, but they may not arbitrarily use their transfer power to undermine the property rights conferred by tenure.

A tenured teacher who is demoted in status or pay as a result of transfer or any adverse change by school authorities is entitled to due process. This is particularly true when a teacher is singled out for a change in assignment, a pay cut, or (upon transfer) a rate of pay less than the rate for others of comparable experience. In such cases, transfers are treated like dismissals, and teachers are entitled to due process of law.

Illinois has incorporated these rights into the state tenure statutes. The law says that when a district transfers a teacher or reduces a teacher's salary, "unless reductions in salary are uniform or based on some reasonable classification, any teacher whose salary is reduced shall be entitled to a notice and a hearing. . . ."[43] Similarly, Washington law invokes notice and hearing rights when a teacher is discharged or "otherwise adversely affected in his or her contract status."[44]

Gibson v. Butler[45]

Carson Riddle held tenure in the Claiborne County, Tennessee, school system when he was made director of the Neighborhood Youth Corps, a federally financed program operated by the school system. The school board, without giving Riddle notice, reassigned him to a principalship at a substantial pay decrease and a substantial increase in transportation expense.

The Tennessee Supreme Court ruled that the board's action was an arbitrary and capricious use of power and that Riddle had been wrongfully demoted. The court ordered the board to restore him to his former position and to compensate him for his loss.

At a time when many school systems are RIFing, pursuing strategies for accumulating certification and seniority can put teachers in line for transfers and reduce their vulnerability. The tenure system, however, may put a crimp on teachers' opportunities for transfer and advancement and, ironically, increase their vulnerability because restrictive tenure areas reduce the pool of positions for which individuals are eligible. Furthermore, in New York, if a teacher wants to transfer or accept promotion to a position in a different tenure area, he or she must give up tenure in the old position and serve a new probation. Teachers in this position not only give up their seniority, they give up their due-process rights for the length of their probation.[46] When New York City officials decided to concentrate staff reductions in the area of guidance, counselors were not allowed to transfer out of the guidance tenure area; they were RIFed on the basis of their seniority as guidance counselors despite their certification and experience in other areas.[47] Louisiana law, in contrast, protects teachers who seek new opportunities: tenured teachers retain tenure in their old positions while they serve probationary terms in the new positions.[48] Should they fail to achieve a new permanent status, their old positions are still protected.

Untenured school administrators are not ordinarily entitled to due process when they are transferred or demoted. In many states, administrators—particularly superintendents—serve at the complete discretion of the board of education. They do not receive tenure as administrators and therefore have no property rights to their positions. However, administrators often receive tenure as certified employees of the school district. If they are dismissed from their administrative positions, they are entitled to other positions commensurate with their qualifications and experience. An Illinois decision is illustrative:

Van Dyke v. Board of Education[49]

Richard Van Dyke was a principal when the school board decided to replace him. Under the Illinois teacher tenure law, a principal does not acquire tenure as a principal but does acquire tenure as a certified employee of a school district. The board transferred Van Dyke to a teaching position at a salary reduction determined by the district's teacher salary schedule.

The court held that the board's action was legal, and that a school board may transfer a principal to a teaching position at a reduced salary "based upon some reasonable classification," provided that the action is bona fide and not "in the nature of chicanery or subterfuge designed to subvert the provisions of the teacher tenure law."

Finally, school authorities may not use their transfer power to interfere with the constitutional rights of teachers or to punish teachers for the exercise of civil rights.[50]

Adcock v. Board of Education[51]

In June 1969, a San Diego high school principal asked the school board to transfer a teacher to a different high school. The teacher, Adcock, had criticized school policies on dress, outside speakers, and student publications.

> At a hearing, the board accepted the argument that Adcock's open and persistent criticism had undermined the authority of the school's staff. The board members agreed that the divisiveness he engendered adversely affected faculty morale and community attitudes toward the school. They transferred him.
>
> Adcock challenged the transfer. The California Supreme Court acknowledged the extensive power of the superintendent, conceding that "a school superintendent has and must have very broad discretion in transferring teachers from one school to another . . . when it in fact is in the best interest of the district (Ed. Code 8-939(c)), and his discretion ordinarily will not be reviewed or interfered with. . . ." However, the court reserved the right to review any transfer that a teacher claimed was motivated by his or her exercise of constitutionally protected rights.
>
> The court finally ruled that the "disharmony" caused by Adcock's criticism was not sufficient to justify his punishment. They noted that his statements had been made at a proper time and place and in a proper manner, that he was trying to use existing means to work for change, and that there had been no disruption. The board's transfer action was ruled invalid.

RIF threatens the job security of teachers in periods of rapid population shifts, economic inflation, and changing educational priorities. Teachers have the right to assurances that RIF will not be used to subvert their tenure rights. Hearing rights, "bumping" rights, access to alternative openings, and the right of return introduce fairness into RIF proceedings and give teachers necessary protection. State statutes and court decisions vary in the specific protection they give RIFed teachers. It is the responsibility of teachers to understand what protection is provided in their state and, if necessary, work for greater protection through the state legislature and courts.

Notes to Chapter 2

1. *Connecticut General Statutes Annotated,* Sec. 10-151.

2. *Illinois Revised Statutes Annotated,* Ch. 122, Sec. 24-12.

3. *New Jersey Statutes Annotated,* Title 18A: 28-9.

4. *Massachusetts General Laws Annotated,* Ch. 71, Sec. 42.

5. *Nutter v. School Committee of Lowell,* 359 N.E. 2d 962 (Mass. App., 1977).

6. *Funston v. District,* 278 P. 1075 (Supreme Ct. of Ore., 1929). See also *Powell v. Board,* 550 P. 2d 1118, 1119 (Supreme Ct. of Wyo., 1976); *Jepsen v. Board,* 153 N.E. 2d 417, 418, 419 (Ill. App., 1958); *Hartman v. Community College,* 270 N.W. 2d 822 (Supreme Ct. of Iowa, 1978).

7. *California Education Code Annotated,* Sec. 13447; *Campbell Elementary Teachers v. Abbott,* 143 Cal. Rptr. 281 (App., 1978).

8. *Phillipi v. District,* 367 A. 2d 1133, 1137 (Pa. Cmwlth., 1977). Although boards have discretion in the first instance to decide on the necessity for RIF, the Supreme Court of Iowa in *Hagarty v. District,* 282 N.W. 2d 92, 98 (1979), wrote, "We could not countenance a subterfuge by which an unscrupulous school board would use a fictitious necessity for staff reduction as a pretext for discharging a teacher." See also *Witt v. School District no. 70,* 273 N.W. 669, 672 (Supreme Ct. of Neb., 1979).

9. *Francisco v. Board,* 525 P. 2d 278 (Wash. App., 1974).

10. *Fedele v. Board of Education,* 394 A. 2d 739 (Ct. of Common Pleas of Conn., 1977).

11. *Stets v. McKeesport,* 350 A. 2d 185 (Pa. Cmwlth., 1976).

12. *Hagopian v. Board of Education,* 372 N. E. 2d 990 (Ill. App., 1978).

13. *Conn. Gen. Stat. Ann.,* Sec. 10-151.

14. *Ill. Rev. Stat. Ann.,* Ch. 122, Sec. 24-12.

15. *Pennsylvania Statutes,* Ch. 24, Sec. 11-1125C.

16. *Calif. Educ. Code Ann.,* Sec. 13447; *Campbell v. Abbott.*

17. *Ohio Revised Code,* Sec. 3319.22 (1978 Supp.).

18. Department of Education, *Ohio Administrative Code,* Ch. 3301-21.

19. *Ill. Rev. Stat. Ann.,* Ch. 122, Sec. 21-1 through 21-25.

20. Illinois Superintendent of Public Instruction, Circular Series A, no. 160. See also *Relph v. Board,* 366 N.E. 2d 1125 (Ill. App., 1977).

21. *Lenard v. Board of Education,* 384 N.E. 2d 1321 (Supreme Ct. of Ill., 1979).

22. There can be little question of the value of delegating to state education authorities the power to revise certification requirements in response to changing educational needs. Obviously, too, school boards have to make decisions within the limits set by the law as they understand it. However, the outrageousness of the Lenard decision should alert teachers to the need to

watch the courts as well as the legislature and state education authorities. In this case the court accepted the proposition that any variation from homeroom instruction constituted departmentalized instruction when in fact the variation was minor and, perhaps, arbitrary. Furthermore, the fact that the commissioner's policy was changed only a year after it was first issued and only months after Lenard's dismissal tends to support Lenard's argument that the new requirements were unreasonable, arbitrary, and discriminatory.

23. *Penn Stat.,* Ch. 24, Sec. 11-1125; See also *Phillipi v. District.*

24. *N.J. Stat. Ann.,* Title 18A: 28-10. Illinois law was recently amended to incorporate seniority in RIF decisions; see *Ill. Rev. Stat. Ann.,* Ch. 122, Sec. 24-12 (Cum. Supp., 1980).

25. *Lascari v. Board,* 116 A. 2d 209 (N.J. Super., 1955).

26. *Tressler v. Upper Dublin,* 373 A. 2d 755, 759 (Pa. Cmwlth., 1977).

27. *Steele v. Board,* 387 N.Y.S. 2d 68 (Ct. of App., 1976). See also *Mitchell v. Board,* 389 N.Y.S. 2d 354 (Ct. of App., 1976).

28. *Peters v. South Kitsap,* 509 P. 2d 6771 (Wash. App., 1973).

29. The Fourteenth Amendment entitles a person to due process in the protection of property. Any deprivation of property—including dismissal during the term of a contract and dismissal of a tenured teacher—entitles a teacher to a hearing. See *Perry v. Sindermann,* 408 U.S. 593 (1972); *Wieman v. Updegraff,* 344 U.S. 183 (1952); and *Connell v. Higginbotham,* 403 U.S. 207 (1971). Whereas many states provide for a hearing for RIFed teachers, some do not. Michigan courts have denied RIFed teachers hearing rights; see *Steeby v. School District,* 224 N.W. 2d 97 (Mich. App., 1974) and *Boyce v. Board,* 257 N.W. 2d 153 (Mich. App., 1977). New York's RIF law has no provision for a hearing; see *Consolidated Laws of New York* (McKinney's), Sec. 2510 (1979) and *Mitchell v. Board.*

30. *Fedele v. Board.*

31. *Baer v. Nyquist,* 357 N.Y. 2d 442 (Ct. of App., 1974).

32. *Glowacki v. Ambach,* 385 N.Y.S. 2d 819 (A.D., 1976).

33. *N.J. Stat. Ann.,* Title 18A: 28-10.

34. *Huettemann v. Board,* 372 N.E. 2d 716 (Ill. App., 1977); *Portage v. Portage,* 368 A. 2d 864, 866 (Pa. Cmwlth., 1977). In North Carolina, tenured teachers have priority for three years, but if they reject positions for which they are certified they lose their priority; see *North Carolina General Statutes,* Sec. 115-142 (1) and (2). New York teachers are placed on a list with a six-year life; see *New York Consolidated Laws,* Sec. 2510 (3) (Cum. Supp., 1979). Tennessee puts no time limits on a RIFed teacher's preferred standing; see *Tennessee Code Annotated,* Sec. 49-1319.

35. *Relph v. Board; Bilek v. Board,* 377 N.E. 2d 1259 (Ill. App., 1978).

36. *Lacy v. Richmond District,* 119 Cal. Rptr. 1 (Supreme Ct., 1975). In *Hagarty v. District,* when a teacher's position as a music teacher was abolished, she was offered a position in social studies for which she was certified. She rejected it. When the music position was fortuitously reinstated, her application was

rejected because board policy allowed a RIFed teacher only one recall right. The court upheld the board's RIF policy.

37. *Englewood v. Englewood,* 375 A. 2d 669 (N.J. Super., 1977).

38. *Illinois Education Association Local v. Board,* 340 N.E. 2d (Supreme Ct. of Ill., 1975). However, a recent amendment to Illinois statutes allows collective-bargaining agreements to take precedence over seniority. Thus, courts may rule that agreements between teachers and school boards which deal with other aspects of RIF also take precedence; see *Ill. Rev. Stat. Ann.,* Ch. 122, Sec. 24-12 (Cum. Supp., 1980). Michigan courts have allowed boards and teacher associations to provide for RIF in their contracts; see *Bruinsma v. Schools,* 197 N.W. 2d 95 (Mich. App., 1972).

39. *Classroom Teachers Association v. Board,* 304 N.E. 2d 516 (Ill. App., 1973).

40. *Bruso v. Board,* 385 N.Y.S. 2d 127 (A.D., 1976).

41. *Peters v. South Kitsap* at 73.

42. Some states give provisional certifications, and some states allow boards to appoint personnel despite the absence of certification. See *Grams v. Melrose-Mindaro District,* 254 N.W. 2d 730 (Supreme Ct. of Wis., 1977).

43. *Ill. Rev. Stat. Ann.,* Ch. 122, Sec. 24-12.

44. *Washington Revised Code Annotated,* Ch. 28A. 58.100.

45. *Gibson v. Butler,* 484 S.W. 2d 356 (Supreme Ct. of Tenn., 1972).

46. *Mitchell v. Board.*

47. *Steele v. Board.*

48. *McCoy v. Tangipahoa Parish Board,* 308 So. 2d 382, 385 (La. App., 1975).

49. *Van Dyke v. Board of Education,* 254, N.E. 2d 76 (Ill. App., 1969).

50. *Tinker v. District,* 393 U.S. 503 (1969); *Finot v. Pasadena Board,* 58 Cal. Rptr. 520 (App., 1967).

51. *Adcock v. Board of Education,* 109 Cal. Rptr. 676 (Supreme Ct., 1973).

3.
NEGLIGENCE

Teachers and school administrators are afraid that they will be accused of negligence whenever a student is injured. They are afraid that they will be held liable for damages and sued for all they are worth.

Most such fears are unrealistic. They are based on misunderstandings of the law and on horror stories passed along the grapevine. This is not to say that teachers need not be vigilant about protecting the safety of their students. For the most part, however, courts have established fair standards for assessing the responsibilities of educators, and some states have granted teachers extraordinary additional legal and financial protection.

The aim of this chapter is to clarify what negligence means for educators. What is negligence? How can a teacher avoid exposing students to unreasonable risk? How do state laws affect the personal liability of the teacher?

Negligence and liability are familiar concepts to most people who have purchased auto and home insurance. Many professional associations, including teachers' associations, offer liability insurance to their members. In layman's terms, *negligence* means *fault:* if it was your fault that damage or an injury occurred, you were negligent. *Liability* means *responsibility:* to be liable means to be legally responsible.

The heart of the problem of negligence is *unreasonable risk*. A negligent person is one who puts another person in unreasonable danger. The critical core of a negligence suit is the possibility of consequences so dangerous that a reasonable person in the same circumstances would anticipate the risk and guard against the consequences.

Cirillo v. Milwaukee[1]

Donald Cirillo, a Milwaukee high school student, was injured during a gym class when a basketball game became a free-for-all. The teacher was not present when the injury occurred. He had left the class of 50 boys unsupervised for 25 minutes.

The court ruled that the teacher had acted unreasonably in leaving 50 boys unsupervised for that amount of time.

There are circumstances, the court reasoned, in which a teacher could anticipate that play would deteriorate. Leaving the students unsupervised contained the seeds of unruliness. *The teacher's presence probably would have prevented the roughhousing that led to Cirillo's injuries. A student testified that the students were watching out for the teacher because they expected him to come back and stop them.*

Thus the teacher was negligent.

Elements of Negligence

There are four elements of negligence: (1) legal duty, (2) failure to conform to a standard of reasonable behavior, (3) cause, and (4) loss.

Legal duty. This term refers to the obligation to protect others, as defined by statutes, rules, and court decisions. It is the duty of every person to refrain from any act that will cause foreseeable harm to others. Duty is established when it can be said that it was foreseeable that an act (or failure to act) would endanger another's interests. For example, an architect has a duty to design a building so that pieces don't fall off and endanger pedestrians. An automobile driver has a duty to signal before making a turn. School employees have a duty to inspect and maintain school facilities and correct situations that may endanger their students.

Everyone has a duty to measure up to the standard of care which would be taken by a reasonable person. However, that standard varies with different circumstances. A teacher who is assigned to monitor the playground during recess is not expected to instruct and observe students with the same diligence as a teacher who coaches boxing; the boxing coach must take more care because the foreseeable danger is greater. When a negligence case is brought before the court, the judge determines, first, if there was a duty and, if so, what would have been a reasonable standard of care.

Failure to meet a standard of reasonable behavior. When this criterion is applied, the actions of the person accused of negligence are compared to an ideal standard of how a reasonable person in the same circumstances would have behaved—behavior that would be generally expected or generally accepted. The normal standard is the standard of the "reasonable person" who is "acting prudently."

The phrases "reasonable person" and "acting prudently" are legal terms. When a negligence case goes to court, the judge uses these phrases in instructing the jury. Generally, it is up to the jury to make the specific determination of whether the defendant's behavior was reasonable in the particular case they are hearing. Juries being what they are, the definition—and therefore the standard—depends on what neighbors, friends, and colleagues expect of the person accused.

In considering whether a person fulfilled his legal duty or met a reasonable standard of behavior, *intentions don't count—actions count.* A person may make an "honest mistake" or may not fully understand the consequences of an act. However, such explanations are not relevant to the legal assessment of negligence. If your actions put another person in danger, and the resultant risk could have been anticipated by a reasonably prudent person, you were negligent—whether or not you meant to be.

Cause. Negligence requires a causal connection between one person's action or inaction and subsequent injury to another. The action must be a "substantial factor" leading to the injury.

If an injury would have occurred no matter what another person did or did not do, that person cannot be held liable for negligence. For example, if a student is injured by a rock thrown into the classroom from the street, the teacher's presence—or absence— could not be considered a causal factor. However, if the danger from the street was foreseeable and supervision or intervention would have prevented the injury, the teacher might be found negligent.

Actual loss or damage. The purpose of a negligence action is to make the injured party whole again by repairing the damage or compensating for the loss. There can be no finding of negligence without proof of real loss.

All four elements of negligence were apparent in the Cirillo case:

- The teacher had a supervisory duty to protect Cirillo. A

reasonable teacher would have foreseen that play might well deteriorate and injuries would occur if 50 boys were left alone in a gym.

• The teacher failed to meet a standard of reasonable behavior by remaining away from the gym for 25 minutes. If it is difficult to imagine 50 boys being quiet and orderly in an unsupervised study hall, it is surely unreasonable to expect them to be quiet and orderly in an unsupervised gym. The teacher should have known better.

• The teacher's absence was more than likely a substantial factor in causing Cirillo's injury. If the teacher had been present, the roughhousing would not have occurred. If he had returned sooner, he might have prevented the injury.

• Finally, Cirillo's losses were real. He required expensive hospital treatment, and he had to make up for his absence from school.

Goals and Risks

The elements of negligence are fixed and unvarying. However, the specific criteria that determine whether each element is present vary greatly from one case to another. In a school setting, the assignment of legal duty and responsibility always represents an effort to balance many conflicting and fluctuating goals.

Education is a social good that the community wants to encourage and support. Teaching students to read and write has a high social priority—higher than driving a car, building a house, or running a factory or a skating rink. Schooling, by bringing together large numbers of children, involves risks. In the interest of education, the community is willing to accept some risks to individuals and property that might not otherwise be tolerated.

Because children may create situations that endanger themselves and others, they need supervision and discipline. School personnel are responsible for controlling the conduct of children in the schools. However, every extra dollar and every extra hour spent on maintaining control over students is lost to the real purpose of the schools. Constant surveillance of students would be not only impossible, but wasteful. Thus, the schools must achieve some compromise level of oversight that protects most of the students most of the time without diverting too many resources from their main function.

If a child gets hurt in school, who should bear the loss? Should the child and the family have to bear the whole burden? Should the teacher, supervisor, or administrator who is responsible for the child's safety in school be held liable? If individual teachers are forced to assume this risk, the field of education will become less attractive. Schools will have to pay higher salaries in order to attract personnel and to defray the costs of individual liability insurance. Generally, the school district and the taxpaying community are in a better position to assume the loss than either the student or the teacher. The availability of liability insurance for school districts spreads the risk still further.

However, some social benefits may result from holding schools and school personnel liable for injuries to students. School employees have been given responsibility for the care and protection of the students. They must maintain the facilities and supervise the students. Diligent planning and inspection can prevent foreseeable injuries. The knowledge that they may be held liable for losses to students may encourage school employees to maintain the safest possible conditions.

Given the conflicting goals of the community, what degree of risk is reasonable? And how can a teacher avoid exposing students to unreasonable risk?

To decide whether the risk in a negligence case was unreasonable, the court must ask and answer several questions:

What were the odds that the victim of negligence would be hurt? If the chance seemed very small, it was reasonable for the teacher to go ahead with the activity. However, as chance of harm or loss increases, the responsibility of the teacher also increases. In a school setting, the chance of harm to students increases as they become involved in more-hazardous activities. Recess and gym are generally considered more hazardous than study hall. Shops and chemistry labs expose students to more-dangerous possibilities than do English or mathematics classes. A field trip presents the possibility of more unknown factors and less control and hence poses greater risks than would be present in the classroom.

The fact that students will be exposed to greater risks as a result of some activity does not mean that the activity should be cancelled. Rather, teachers and school administrators must take more than normal care in planning and supervising the activity.

***Thompson v. Board of the City of New York*[2]**
Helen Thompson, 14, fell down the school stairs during
class dismissal when she was pushed by a boy running down

behind her. The principal was accused of negligence for "allowing overcrowding to take place and to permit roughing by large boys, wholly without any supervision whatsoever."

The Court of Appeals of New York reviewed the principal's dismissal procedures. These included regular conferences with teachers, rules for teacher oversight of dismissal, regular inspection of halls and stairways, personal observation, and supervision of teachers and students.

The court held that the principal had "exercised such general supervision as was possible. . . . [He] could not personally attend to each class at the same time, nor was any such duty imposed upon him." He had not been negligent.

Titus v. Lindberg[3]

Robert Titus, 9, was hit in the eye by a paper clip shot by another student, Richard Lindberg.

The injury occurred while he was waiting for the school doors to open. Although the Fairview school did not officially open until 8:15 a.m., it was customary for students to arrive at school grounds at about 8:00 a.m. The Fairview students were joined by older students who waited to be bused to other schools.

The New Jersey Supreme Court found that the school principal "had not announced any rules with respect to the congregation of his students and their conduct prior to entry into the classrooms. He had assigned none of the teachers or other school personnel to assist him. . . . He then failed to take any measures toward overseeing their presence and activities. . . ."

The court held that the students' conduct was reasonably to be anticipated and guarded against. It concluded that inadequate supervision was a cause of the injury. The court ruled that the principal had been negligent.

How much harm could foreseeably come to the victim? A blow to the ego? A scratch? Loss of a limb? Death? If the amount of foreseeable harm is very small, it is reasonable to ignore it. However, as students engage in more-dangerous activities involving physical exertion, machinery, or chemicals, the threat to limb and life increases. Thus it is necessary to take greater safety precautions and supervise activities more closely.

Miller v. Griesel[4]

William Miller, a fifth-grade student, was cut and blinded when a detonator cap blew up in his face. Another student had brought the device to school in a tackle box and had offered to trade it for some pencils.

The incident occurred at recess, during which time students were allowed to remain in their classrooms. School rules permitted teachers to leave the classrooms during recess if they could arrange for another teacher to "look in" on the students. Another teacher had agreed and had looked in on the students.

In its decision, the Supreme Court of Indiana expressed its belief that, even though "persons entrusted with children, or others whose characteristics make it likely that they may do somewhat unreasonable things, have a special responsibility recognized by the common law to supervise their charges," schools are not expected to absolutely ensure the safety of their pupils. The trial court dismissed the suit when Miller "failed to show the actual length of time the students were left unattended, that the activity in which they were engaged was particularly hazardous, or that any of the students in the room were of a troublesome, mischievous nature. . . ."

Station v. Teachers Insurance[5]

Geraldine Station was burned when an alcohol burner exploded. The burner was part of a science fair exhibit set up by a science teacher and another eighth-grade student. The students were trying to relight it when it blew up.

The Louisiana court ruled that a dangerous instrument had been placed in the hands of children without any special degree of care, supervision, or direction. The teacher had failed to alert the students to the dangerous nature of the alcohol. Further, the teacher did not positively warn them not to relight the burner should it go out—even though he could have anticipated that it would go out, since it had malfunctioned on prior occasions. The teacher was found to have been negligent.

Was the harm avoidable through foresight? A reasonably prudent person can guard against only those dangers that he or others can anticipate. Thus, there must be some reason for or warning of danger. Furthermore, only a person who was in a position to prevent harm to the victim can be held liable.

The question of preventability invariably arises in cases involving lapses in supervision: If the teacher had been there, would his presence have prevented the events which led to the injury, or could the teacher have intervened to stop the events? (This is sometimes referred to as the "but for" standard: Would the injury have occurred *but for* the absence of the teacher?)

The courts have handled this question in two ways. First, they have questioned the duration of the events: Was the harm caused by a single impulsive act, or was it preceded by a series of similar dangerous acts? In the Cirillo case, the court noted that the injury did not occur until after a lengthy period of horseplay. In the Titus case, the court's belief that supervision might have prevented the injury was strengthened by the knowledge that Lindberg had shot a second student with a paper clip five minutes before Titus was injured. Thus, *but for* the absence of the teacher, Cirillo or Titus would not have been harmed.

Second, the courts have looked at the instrument that caused the injury: Was it a common item, one generally found in the possession of students and not easily identified as a potential threat? Or was it clearly identifiable as being imminently dangerous? Courts have been sympathetic to teachers when student injuries have been caused by pencils, rulers, pointers, balls, fingers, or fists. Normal supervisory diligence would not lead a teacher to anticipate danger from these familiar articles, and the presence or absence of the teacher is irrelevant. However, when the injury was caused by an article that a teacher would immediately identify as dangerous—for example, a knife—the presence of the teacher becomes a crucial factor.

Christofides v. Hellenic Eastern Orthodox Church[6]

At the Hellenic Church school, students were required to report to the classroom at 8:30 a.m.; the teacher did not arrive until 8:55. During that time most of the students engaged in horseplay, fighting and chasing one another. One student brandished a knife for five or ten minutes and then stabbed a fellow student, Alexander Christofides.

The court noted that the stabbing "was not a momentary, sudden, impulsive, or instantaneous one without prior warning." There was a warning period during which the knife was in view. Had the teacher been present, he would have been in a position to halt the imminent threat. His presence might have prevented the stabbing. He was found to be negligent.

What was the expected standard of conduct? Generally, the defendant's behavior is measured against actions which would be taken by a reasonable person of ordinary prudence. The "reasonable person" is a mythical being who personifies the community's ideal of reasonable behavior. Traditionally, the courts have allowed professionals to set their own standards. For example, doctors are expected to have the skill and learning commonly possessed by competent members of their profession. The standard of conduct for doctors is "good medical practice"—which is to say, whatever is customary and usual in the profession.

Teachers are expected to follow good educational and supervisory practices. Thus, it makes sense for teachers and school officials to formalize supervisory expectations rather than to leave them to common sense and custom. Once a set of guidelines has been formalized, the absence of a supervisory requirement can be used as a defense—no need was foreseen by reasonable people. In addition, if an injury occurs despite reasonable precautions, the fact that formalized standards exist suggests that the injury could not have been anticipated or avoided.

Of course, courts and juries may reject professional standards that offer insufficient protection to the public. Furthermore, it is not a defense to say that negligence occurred during the performance of mandatory or authorized acts. No one can be authorized to place another in unreasonable risk of injury.

What standards determine reasonable supervision? As we have tried to suggest, there is no easy answer. Rather, a series of factors combine to make a teacher's behavior seem more or less reasonable. The courts have rejected the idea that a teacher can or should give personal attention to every student at all times. The courts have accepted the proposition that a school has a duty to protect students under its supervision regardless of the location of the accident, the fault of the student in causing his own injury, and the involvement of a third party. These factors may, however, mitigate or entirely eliminate the liability of the school.

Banks v. Terrebonne Parish School Board[7]

Kevin Banks was injured when he practiced tumbling before his gym class. The coach had expressly forbidden such tumbling; had he been aware of the activity, he would have stopped it. Unfortunately, the coach was occupied with collecting valuables and other classroom preliminaries when Banks was injured.

The Louisiana Appeals Court ruled that the coach could not at one and the same time observe all actions of all

*students in his class. Nor would such comprehensive observa-
tion have been possible short of providing a supervisor for
each student. Thus, the coach was not negligent.*

Caltavuturo v. Passaic[8]

*Salvatore Caltavuturo, a 12-year-old student in a
Passaic, New Jersey, elementary school, was dismissed for
lunch. He and some other boys took a shortcut through a
playground fence. Salvatore cut his leg on a jagged portion
of the fence and eventually developed a permanent bone
disease as a result of the injury.*

*The school playground was owned by the city. The city
had installed the fence but had difficulty maintaining it.
Children cut new holes as soon as it was repaired.*

*The principal had teachers stationed in the playground
to observe the students as they left and returned to school.
However, Caltavutura was a patrol guard; he stayed at
school longer than most of the other students. When the
accident occurred, the teachers had already left their posts
for their own quick lunches.*

*The principal knew that children used the holes in the
fence and considered it a problem, but he had taken no
remedial action.*

*The New Jersey Supreme Court ruled that it is the duty
of school personnel to exercise reasonable supervisory care
for the safety of students. The evidence properly presented a
triable jury question on the issue of the principal's
negligence.*

Hoyem v. Manhattan Beach[9]

*Michael Hoyem, 10, left summer school in the middle of
the school day without the knowledge or permission of
school authorities. He was hit by a motorcycle at a public
intersection.*

*The California Supreme Court ruled that a school
district has a duty to supervise students on school premises
and may be held liable for injuries which are caused by the
district's failure to exercise reasonable care. In this case, the
duty owed to the student is not lessened by the facts that the
student left without permission, that he was attending a
voluntary summer school, and that the direct source of his
injuries was a negligent motorist.*

*Students have been wandering off from school since the
days of Huck Finn. The duty to supervise is a recognition of
the fact that "students will not always conduct themselves in*

*accordance with school rules or as safely as they ought to.
We cannot say that Michael's departure from school was
unforeseeable or that the risk was not created by the school's
failure to exercise care in supervising its pupils."*

*Thus the jury had to decide: Did the school exercise
reasonable supervisory care? Was an injury of the general
type that occurred foreseeable? But for negligent supervision,
would the injury have occurred? Comparatively, what
proportion of responsibility must be borne by the negligent
motorist?*

The Role of State Law

Many states have laws that modify the impact of normal negligence proceedings on schools and teachers. Chief among these is the
law of sovereign immunity. In states with sovereign immunity, or the
"doctrine of lack of statutory consent," a citizen may not sue the
state without legislative permission. These states generally extend
immunity to municipalities and school districts.

Sovereign immunity is a potentially disastrous law for teachers
and other people who work for government agencies. Under normal
circumstances, the victim of negligence would sue the employer of
the negligent agent as the party who is both ultimately responsible
and best able to compensate for the loss. However, if the employer is
cloaked in immunity, only the employer's agents can be sued. In
fact, sovereign immunity has discouraged suits altogether, since most
teachers and other government workers possess only modest assets.
The elimination of sovereign immunity probably would be
advantageous to both teachers and victims of genuine negligence.

Most states have abandoned strict sovereign immunity in favor
of alternatives that are less harsh for the victims of negligence.[10] Less
than a dozen states retain absolute immunity for local governments,
and even these states allow some exceptions. The alternatives to
immunity generally increase the responsibilities of the school district
and protect the teacher. The major statutory alternative is to
authorize local school districts to purchase liability insurance, with a
waiver of immunity up to the limits of the insurance. For example, a
provision of the Kansas education law reads:

> The board of education of any school district of the state
> securing insurance as hereinbefore authorized thereby waives
> its governmental immunity from liability for any damage by

reason of death or injury to persons or property proximately caused by the negligent acts of any officer, teacher or employee of such school district when acting within the scope of his authority or within the course of his employment. Such immunity shall be waived only to the extent of the insurance so obtained.[11]

Some states—among them Florida, Georgia, Iowa, New Jersey, Vermont, West Virginia, and New York—have adopted "save harmless" statutes to protect school employees.[12] Such laws enable schools to indemnify the costs incurred by teachers in defending themselves against negligence suits. The New Jersey law reads:

Whenever any civil action has been or shall be brought against any person holding any office, position or employment under the jurisdiction of any board of education, for any act or omission arising out of and in the course of the performance of the duties of such office, *the board shall defray all costs of defending such action, including reasonable counsel fees and expenses,* together with costs of appeal, if any, and shall save harmless and protect such person from any financial loss resulting therefrom; and said board may arrange for and maintain appropriate insurance to cover all such damages, losses and expenses.[13]

Florida law similarly authorizes school boards to provide legal services for officers and employees charged with actions arising out of the performance of assigned duties or responsibilities. Apparently, however, these services are available only to innocent employees; an employee who pleads guilty or nolo contendere or is found guilty must reimburse the board. Whereas the New Jersey and Florida laws appear to *require* school boards to compensate employees, under Georgia law they *may* do it. The Georgia law authorizes school boards "in their discretion, to purchase policies of liability insurance or contracts of indemnity insuring . . . superintendents, teachers, principals and other administrators and employees against damages arising out of the performance of their duties."[14] Further, Georgia boards may adopt policies to assume the defense of employees against all or specified civil or criminal actions arising out of performance of their duties.

In a seminal article on teacher liability written in 1959, Paul O. Proehl noted that the great majority of teacher negligence cases came from states that had eliminated sovereign immunity and allowed direct action against school governing units.[15] He identified

California, New York, and Washington as these states, adding:

> Only a very few cases go to the appellate level in other states,
> including those which provide for indemnification of the
> teacher, indicating a reluctance, born no doubt of hopeless-
> ness rather than sympathy, to proceed against teachers. It
> may be, on the other hand, that this imbalance results from a
> less rigorous application of the fault principle in jurisdictions
> whose statutes allow suit against the school, and a tendency
> by their courts to treat the statute as one *making the school
> the insurer.* There are cases which point in this direction,
> despite statements therein to the contrary, and verdicts favor-
> able to the plaintiff are more frequent in these jurisdictions.[16]

As an increasing number of states have abolished sovereign
immunity, more suits have been filed in more states. California and
New York still appear to be far and away the leaders and to have
gone furthest toward a "less rigorous application of the fault
principle."

Rather than entirely abandoning sovereign immunity, the legislatures and courts of a number of states have attempted to limit it by
distinguishing among government functions and types of negligent
acts. One such distinction is made between proprietary or business
functions and strictly governmental functions.[17] Functions that can
be performed only by government are generally immune from
liability: governments are not liable for their laws and regulations,
enforcement of the laws, or failure to enforce the laws. A proprietary function is one that could just as easily be performed by a
private company. In this kind of role, government is held to the same
standard of liability as a private company. Examples of proprietary
functions include municipal utilities, transportation, parking, and
garbage collection. Sometimes the distinction between governmental
and proprietary functions depends on whether the provider makes a
profit (revenue) from the service.

Critics of immunity have sought to make government responsible for its negligence when it performs proprietary functions. Why,
they ask, should a private operator of a school-bus service be liable
while a school district that operates its own buses is immune? Why
should a school be immune from liability when it rents out its gym,
auditorium, stadium or buses? Although some states, among them
Delaware, Nebraska, and Virginia, have allowed suits in connection
with proprietary functions, other states—Alabama, Idaho, Indiana,

Oregon, and Pennsylvania among them—have specifically rejected the distinction as being too difficult to determine.[18] Nevertheless, even those states most committed to immunity—for example, Missouri, Ohio, and South Carolina—have waived immunity in cases involving state-operated cars and buses. In a number of states, school district liability is limited to causes of action arising from the use of motor vehicles.[19]

A second distinction, more pertinent to school people, is made between unintentional negligence and negligence that is intentional, or reckless, or willful and wanton. Statutes in several states seek to protect government workers from liability for unintentional negligence committed while performing tasks that are within the scope of their duties, but they do not protect a worker whose negligence is willful and wanton. For example, a Connecticut statute reads:

> Each board of education shall protect and save harmless any member of such board or any teacher . . . and the managing board of any public school . . . shall protect and save harmless any member of such boards, or any teacher or other employee thereof . . . from financial loss and expense, including legal fees and costs, if any, arising out of any claim, demand, suit or judgment by reason of alleged negligence . . . which acts are not wanton, reckless or malicious, provided such teacher . . . was acting in the discharge of his or her duties or within the scope of employment.[20]

Similarly, Florida law provides that the state may authorize the legal defense of officers or employees sued for negligent acts within the scope of employment in the absence of wanton or willful misconduct.[21]

The "willful and wanton" distinction has played a key role in school negligence cases in Illinois. Illinois law reads:

> Teachers and other certified educational employees shall maintain discipline in the schools. . . . In all matters relating to the discipline in and conduct of the schools and the school children they stand in the relation of parents and guardians to the pupils. This relationship shall extend to all activities connected with the school program and may be exercised at any time for the safety and supervision of the pupils in the absence of their parents or guardians.[22]

The Illinois Supreme Court has ruled that this statute places educators in the same relation to students as parents to their children.[23] The relationship extends to student discipline and conduct and all school-related activities. Under Illinois law, parents are not liable for injuries to their children unless there is evidence of willful and wanton misconduct. Thus, the court has ruled that teachers cannot be held liable for injuries suffered as a result of a supervisory failure unless it can be shown that the teacher intended to harm the student. The practical effect of this law is that it is almost impossible to find an Illinois teacher negligent.[24]

The situation in Texas is substantially similar. A professional school employee is not personally liable for acts performed within the scope of employment and which involve the exercise of judgment or discretion, except in circumstances where excessive force or negligence results in physical injury to the student. Thus, teacher liability is limited to cases involving the use of excessive force to punish students.[25]

A distinction of even greater significance to school people is the distinction between supervision of students and maintenance of physical facilities and equipment. In legal language, this is the distinction between discretionary acts and ministerial acts. Discretionary acts are acts of judgment; they require thought, evaluation, and decision. Ministerial acts are administrative duties, requiring only obedience to orders or performance of duties specified by law in terms of time, place, and manner. Of course, this distinction also tends to break down in the context of real situations: few "ministerial" acts do not involve at least some discretion in the way they are carried out.

The supervisory function performed by school administrators and teachers is generally discretionary. School authorities must evaluate the potential dangers of numerous situations and decide on the allocation of supervisory resources. Since school personnel cannot be everywhere at once, there are bound to be lapses in supervision. Discretion plays a role and justifies these lapses.

By contrast, the maintenance of school facilities is a ministerial function. School authorities are expected to maintain facilities in working order and to eliminate dangerous conditions. No judgment or decision can justify dangerous stairways, broken playground equipment, or poorly fitting football gear. School people are no less liable than businesses when they expose their clientele to dangerous facilities and equipment.

The distinction between discretionary acts and ministerial acts has been recognized in statutes and court decisions. A Georgia statute exempts municipal corporations from liability for failure of performance or errors in performing their legislative and judicial functions.[26] However, they are liable for unskillful performance of their duties. In New Hampshire, the state supreme court has abolished immunity for municipalities except for acts and omissions constituting (a) the exercise of legislative and judicial functions and (b) the exercise of executive or planning functions involving the making of basic policy decisions.[27] Similarly, the Illinois Supreme Court has ruled that teacher immunity extends only to unintentional negligence which results from a discretionary act.

Gerrity v. Beatty[28]

A Downers Grove (Illinois) High School sophomore, Matthew Patrick Gerrity, suffered severe injuries while making a tackle in a junior varsity football game. In court, he claimed that the equipment assigned to him was inadequate, ill fitting, and defective. The coach, in the exercise of ordinary care, either knew or should have known of the faulty condition of the equipment.

The Illinois Supreme Court distinguished this case from prior negligence cases that alleged failure of supervision. The prior cases, the court said, arose out of the teacher/student relationship in matters relating to the teacher's personal supervision and control of the conduct or physical movement of the student. Public policy considerations supported the teacher's broad discretion and latitude in controlling students. Here the reverse was true: public policy considerations argued "rather strongly against any interpretation which relaxes a school district's obligation to insure equipment provided for students. . . . To hold school districts to the duty of ordinary care in such matters would not be unduly burdensome. . . ."

In summary, negligence is the failure to anticipate unreasonable risk and guard against the consequences. Teachers must be concerned for the safety of their students. Students are immature; they lack experience and judgment. Teachers must use their superior understanding to anticipate dangerous situations and protect students. Teachers who plan for the safety of their students and take precautions on the basis of a realistic assessment of risk have little to fear.

In general, teachers are unlikely to be held responsible for students' injuries. Normal considerations of negligence and liability protect the responsible teacher. Furthermore, some states effectively immunize teachers—even negligent teachers—from legal responsibility and financial loss. Even sovereign immunity—which, in the abstract, makes teachers the only available targets for suits—probably deters suits. Exceptions to sovereign immunity allow the school to replace the teacher as the primary focus of legal actions.

Notes to Chapter 3

1. *Cirillo v. Milwaukee*, 150 N.W. 2d 460 (Supreme Ct. of Wis., 1967).

2. *Thompson v. Board of the City of New York*, 280 N.Y. 92 (Ct. of App., 1939), 19 N.E. 2d 796.

3. *Titus v. Lindberg*, 228 A. 2d 65 (Supreme Ct. of N.J., 1967).

4. *Miller v. Griesel*, 308 N.E. 2d 701 (Supreme Ct. of Ind., 1974).

5. *Station v. Teachers Insurance*, 292 So. 2d 289 (La. App., 1974). See also *Ressel v. Board*, 395 N.Y.S. 2d 263 (A.D., 1977), wherein the court held that a jury could reasonably assess the knowledge, experience, and conduct of a 16-year-old victim of a shop accident.

6. *Christofides v. Hellenic Eastern Orthodox Church*, 227 N.Y.S. 2d 946 (N.Y.C. Munic. Ct., 1962).

7. *Banks v. Terrebonne Parish School Board*, 339 So. 2d. 1295 (La. App., 1976).

8. *Caltavuturo v. Passaic*, 307 A. 2d 114 (N.J. Super., 1973).

9. *Hoyem v. Manhattan Beach*, 150 Cal. Rptr. 1 (Supreme Ct., 1978).

10. There have been radical changes in the status of sovereign immunity over the period of the last 20 years. Abrogation and modifications of sovereign immunity have been precipitated by both courts and state legislatures. Teachers should examine the particular laws of their state governing teacher negligence and liability and school-district immunity. For a state-by-state review of the status of governmental immunity, see P.A. Harley and B.E. Wassinger, "Governmental Immunity: Despotic Mantle or Creature of Necessity," *Washburn Law Review* 16, no. 1 (1976), pp. 12-53; also W. Prosser, *Handbook of the Law of Facts*, 4th ed. (St. Paul: West Publishing Co., 1974), Sec. 131 at 985, 986.

11. *Kansas Statutes Annotated*, Sec. 72-8404. Also see *North Carolina General Statutes*, Sec. 115-53 (1979 Supp.); *Florida Statutes Annotated*, Sec. 234.03(4);

Minnesota Statutes Annotated, Sec. 466.06 (1977). A local government's purchase of insurance does not automatically waive the defense of governmental immunity. See *Beiser v. Parkway School District,* 589 S.W. 2d 277 (Supreme Ct. of Mo., 1979) and *Pichette v. Mastique Public Schools,* 269 N.W. 2d 143 (Supreme Ct. of Mich., 1978). Nevertheless, despite lack of legislative authorization, some courts have held that the purchase of insurance represents a waiver. These courts have reasoned that, since the local government had insurance and the public had already paid the premiums, the usual objections to suits were not relevant. The immunity defense only benefited the insurance company. See Prosser, *Handbook of the Law,* Sec. 131 at 985.

12. *Fla. Stat. Ann.,* Ch. 230, Sec. 234. Also see ibid., Ch. 232, Sec. 275; *Talmadge v. Board,* 355 So. 2d 502 (Fla. App., 1978); *Georgia Code Annotated,* Ch. 32-850, 851, 852; *New Jersey Statutes Annotated,* Title 18A: 16-6; *Vermont Statutes Annotated,* Sec. 1756; *Virginia Code Annotated,* Sec. 8-12-7.

13. *N.J. Stat. Ann.,* Title 18A: 16-6.

14. *Ga. Code Ann.,* Ch. 32-850-852. Also see *N.C. Gen. Stat.,* Sec. 115-53.1 (1979 Supp.).

15. P.O. Proehl, "Tort Liability of Teachers," *Vanderbilt Law Review* 12 (1959), pp. 723-754.

16. Ibid., pp. 741, 742.

17. Harley and Wassinger identify a number of statutes and court decisions in various states dealing with the governmental/proprietary distinction. See also Prosser, *Handbook of the Law,* Sec. 131 at 979 and *Owen v. City of Independence,* _____ U.S. _____ 100 S. Ct. 1398 (1980).

18. In *Administrative Law Text,* 3rd ed. (St. Paul: West Publishing Co., 1972), K.C. Davis writes that the governmental/proprietary distinction "became one of the most unsatisfactory known to law" and a cause of confusion. Prosser (Sec. 131 at 982) writes of this and other distinctions: "There is little that can be said about such distinctions except that they exist, that they are highly artificial, and that they make no great amount of sense. Obviously this is an area in which the law has sought in vain for some reasonable and logical compromise, and has ended with a pile of jackstraws."
    Perhaps it would be best to view the governmental/proprietary distinction in terms of justification. "Governmental" is a designation the courts give to functions that they decide the government should be able to perform without having to compensate citizens who are adversely affected. Of course, this designation reflects sound policy judgment. See discussion in *Pichette v. Mastique* at 147.

19. *Texas Tort Claims Act,* Sec. 19A, 1970. *Texas Revised Civil Statutes Annotated* (Vernon's), Art. 6252-19, Sec. 19A (1976-77 Supp.).

20. *Connecticut General Statutes Annotated,* Sec. 10-235 (Cum. Supp., 1979).

21. *Fla. Stat. Ann.,* Ch. 230, Sec. 234.

22. *Illinois Revised Statutes Annotated,* Ch. 122, Sec. 24-24, 34-84a.

23. *Kobylanski v. Chicago Board,* 347, N.E. 2d 705 (Supreme Ct. of Ill., 1976). See also Charles R. Winkler, "Tort Immunity of Teachers and School

Districts," *Illinois Bar Journal,* March 1977, pp. 456, 461, 462.

24. Liability of teachers is not impossible. See *Baikie v. Luther High School South,* 368 N.E. 2d 542 (Ill. App. 1977) and *Gerrity v. Beatty,* 373 N.E. 2d 1323 (Supreme Ct. of Ill. 1978).

25. *Barr v. Bernhard,* 562 S.W. 2d 844, 849 (Supreme Ct. of Texas, 1978).

26. *Ga. Code Ann.,* Sec. 69-301. This distinction does not appear in the statute authorizing schools to purchase insurance.

27. *Merrill v. Manchester,* 33 A. 2d 378 (Supreme Ct. of N.H., 1974).

28. *Gerrity v. Beatty.* See also *Thomas v. Chicago Board,* 377 N.E. 2d 55 (Ill. App., 1978); *Pavlik v. Kinsey,* 259 N.W. 2d 709 (Supreme Ct. of Wis., 1977). For additional details see Prosser, "Defamation," in *Handbook of the Law,* Sec. 106, 110.

4.
MALPRACTICE AND DEFAMATION

Malpractice and defamation, as bases of suits against teachers, are an ironic duo. A malpractice suit generally constitutes a claim that the school failed to fulfill its responsibilities to educate a child: the school passed the student along despite the student's failure to master material and perform at an acceptable level. School authorities failed to diagnose the student's problems and failed to address the root causes of failure. The school did not provide a compensatory program. A defamation suit constitutes a claim that the school ruined a child's good name. How? The teacher exposed the fact that the student had failed to perform up to a given standard. The teacher tried to deal with the causes of the student's failures. The student's record includes statements about these failures.

Educational Malpractice

To many educators, it must appear that the tide of public regard has turned against professionals. Learned practitioners who once were appreciated for their services now are sued for malpractice. Where people once blamed the fates or themselves for their condition, now they blame those who come to their aid. We have progressed from charges of medical malpractice to legal malpractice and now educational malpractice. Educational malpractice, however, is an idea whose time has come mainly in the press rather than in the courts.

Educational malpractice is a specific form of negligence accusation. Malpractice suits are based on the failures of apparently normal students to attain average levels of achievement in school. Schools are accountable for supervisory failures that lead to physical injuries to students. Why not also hold the schools responsible for negligent teaching that results in students' ignorance?

Those who believe that there is such a thing as educational malpractice argue that school boards, administrators, and teachers are responsible for negligent acts that lead to injuries. Students who graduate without the ability to read or compute are surely as crippled as those who break their necks. Thus, teachers, counselors, psychologists, and administrators who fail to educate students are every bit as negligent as those who fail to adequately supervise the physical safety of students.

The courts have refused to consider that the normal academic relationship of teachers and students falls within the orbit of negligence. Basically, they have rejected the proposition that educational malpractice involves the essential elements of negligence. They have stressed that the schools have no legal *duty of care* for the academic achievement of their students. In addition, the courts have ruled that there are formidable philosophical and practical barriers to determining whether instruction has been adequate, whether a student has suffered an academic injury, and whether there is a causal connection between quality of instruction and academic injury.

Peter W. v. San Francisco Unified School District[1]

Peter W. attended San Francisco schools for 12 years. He graduated at the age of 18 with a fifth-grade reading ability. His ability to hold a job and his earning capacity were limited by his inability to read or write. He had a permanent disability that might be improved by compensatory tutoring.

In court, Peter's attorney attempted to demonstrate that the school district, administrators, and teachers had negligently and carelessly:

• Failed to apprehend Peter's reading disabilities.

• Assigned him to classes in which he could not read the books and other materials.

• Allowed him to pass from one grade level to the next without having mastered the skills needed to succeed or benefit from subsequent courses.

• Assigned him to classes in which the instructors were unqualified or which were not geared to his reading level.

> • *Permitted him to graduate from high school and
> thereby deprived him of additional instruction, even though
> California law requires an eighth-grade reading level for
> graduation.*

Edward Donohue v. Copiague Union School District [2]
*When Edward Donohue graduated from the Copiague
(New York) School District, he did not have basic reading
and writing skills. In order to acquire these skills, he had to
seek private tutoring.*

*In court, Donohue's attorney argued that the school had
a duty of care to instruct him in the various academic subjects, evaluate his learning capacity and ability, and, essentially, to see that he gained sufficient comprehension of subjects to achieve passing grades and obtain a Certificate of
Graduation. He argued further that because Edward
Donohue had not mastered basic skills, the school and its
agents, servants, and employees had breached their duty to
him in that they had:*
• *Given him passing grades.*
• *Failed to evaluate or test his mental ability or his
ability to learn.*
• *Failed to provide adequate facilities, teachers, or
psychologists.*
• *Failed to teach him in such a manner that he could
learn.*
• *Practiced methods that were defective and not up to
the standards of other high schools in the county.*

The courts in both New York and California rejected the education malpractice suits. All the courts that heard the two suits cited
similar reasons for rejecting them.

Duty of Care

The courts require a negligence suit to *state a cause of action.*
This means simply that the person who sues must demonstrate the
presence of the four conditions of negligence: duty of care, failure to
fulfill the duty of care, injury, and cause. In dismissing educational
malpractice suits, courts have ruled that the suits failed to establish
the existence of these conditions. Primarily, the suits failed to show
that the schools owed the students a *duty of care.* Duty of care, the
courts say, is the sum total of considerations of policy which lead the
law to say that the particular plaintiff is entitled to compensation.

Does the school have a duty of care to students relative to academic instruction and student academic achievement? The courts say "No." Courts have not, in the past, recognized (and, for the present, refuse to recognize) such a duty of care. This position is dictated by a host of public policy considerations, administrative difficulties, and practical problems.

To determine if there is a duty of care, the courts must take into account a large number of policy considerations. These considerations can be examined by asking the following questions about a particular educational malpractice suit:

• Was the student's injury foreseeable? Negligence is the failure of a prudent person to guard against foreseeable injury. There is no negligence without a foreseeable chance of injury. Can we expect the schools to foresee and guard against the possibility that some students may fail?

How certain is it that the student suffered an injury? There is no negligence without actual injury or damage. If the injury is surrounded by ambiguity—difficult to see, touch, measure—it is difficult to support negligence action. Additionally, how can it be said that students have suffered injury when they fail to achieve some average level of academic competence? By definition, some students will always be below the average.

• How close is the connection between the actions of school personnel and the injury to the student? Negligence requires a direct causal link between the action of the negligent person and injury to the victim. Can it be said that the actions of a teacher or several teachers caused a student not to learn to read or write? But for the poor performance of the school, would the student be at least a normal achiever?

• Should the school accept moral blame for the student's condition? One idea behind negligence law is to pass on the victim's loss to the one who was responsible. While the characteristics of a school may be a factor in a student's failure, can it really be said that school personnel are to blame?

• Would imposing a duty of care on the school prevent future harm to other students? Liability is therapeutic. One reason for imposing liability is to reform negligent and irresponsible behavior. If courts accepted educational malpractice, could the schools prevent similar future injuries and suits?

• What burden will the school and the community bear if the courts impose a duty and liability for breach of duty? What are the costs? Is there insurance that could spread the costs? There is no point in imposing liability if the costs cannot or will not be accepted by the taxpayers who support schools.

Taking these policy considerations into account, the courts have concluded that schools have no duty of care for the academic success of their students.

Although there are no court precedents for a duty of care, the attorneys for both Peter W. and Donohue argued that state statutes established standards of care. The *California Education Code* has several provisions that require the schools to (1) design courses of study which meet the needs of pupils, (2) instruct students in the basic skills of reading and writing, and (3) award high school graduation certificates only to students who have demonstrated proficiency in basic skills. New York's education laws require school authorities to test underachievers and to determine whether pupils can benefit from special educational programs.

The courts, however, held that these obligations were not designed to protect against the risk of injury to students. Rather, they are administrative; they are directed toward the attainment of optimum educational results. Whereas failure to comply with these mandates does not impose liability, such statutes do provide a basis for students and their parents to seek remedies from the school and from higher levels of state school administration.

Practical Considerations

In addition to policy considerations, some practical problems have led the courts to reject claims of educational malpractice. These problems involve the remaining three elements of the legal definition of negligence.

Workability of a standard of care. Although pedagogy is called a science by some, it is, at best, an art. The courts recognize that it is impossible for professional educators to develop programs that ensure academic achievement. Further, they are convinced that the courts cannot and should not get involved in defining good teaching. Thus, there is no workable standard of care to which the courts can hold schools or teachers.

Certainty of injury. Liability law is designed to compensate persons who have been negligently injured. The presumption is that people have been damaged by such injuries. They have lost arms, legs, eyes. They may not be able to work or to engage in enjoyable leisure activities. They may have had to pay for doctors, medicine, or prosthetic devices. The purpose of liability settlements is to make damaged people whole again—to reestablish the conditions that existed before they were harmed by the negligent acts of others.

The laws providing for systems of public schools are designed to confer benefits on society. They offer to children the opportunity to attend school. Most students enter school in a condition of academic ignorance. If they are still ignorant when they leave, have they been injured or damaged by the school?

Almost every person achieves some level of reading, writing, and computing ability. Some people achieve much higher levels than others. Clearly, these skills are linked to careers and career opportunities. If a graduate's skills are adequate for a job as a plumber or bricklayer but not for a career as a teacher or data analyst, has that person been injured by the schools?

While there may be some connection between high school academic achievement and career choice, happiness, success, or wealth, such relationships are statistical at best. The outcome of any single person's long march through life is uncertain. How, then, can a particular student's academic failure be construed as an injury if there is no basis for predicting that it will inevitably have a negative impact on his or her life, or that academic success will ensure health, wealth, and happiness?

Causal connection. Too many factors intervene between a school and a particular student for the courts to assign a cause-and-effect relationship to academic failure. A student's home life, street life, intelligence, drive, and health—all affect learning and achievement. How can a school be responsible for a student's academic achievement when it has no control over the student outside the classroom, and when what is taught in the classroom is a minor component of the total number of factors that account for learning and achievement?

The Potential for Malpractice

Although the courts have rejected educational malpractice as a basis for liability, they have not ruled out other types of negligence suits against schools and educators. As noted in Chapter 3, the courts are willing to entertain suits based on physical injuries that result from allegedly negligent supervision. Many states now assume that schools have a duty of care for the physical safety of students in their charge. In this context, the criteria for negligence are easily applicable to a school setting.

What about psychological injury? Courts have accepted the possibility that injury may be more than skin deep; people may suffer psychological damage as the result of negligent actions. It is conceivable that a student might be psychologically impaired as a result of the negligence of school personnel.

Finally, the New York Court of Appeals, even though it unanimously rejected Donohue's appeal, appeared to leave the door open for the possibility that educational malpractice might theoretically fall within the traditional interpretations of negligence law. Four of the six judges affirming the Donohue decision admitted this possibility:

> Thus, the imagination need not be overly taxed to envision allegations of a legal duty of care flowing from educators, if viewed as professionals, to their students. If doctors, lawyers, architects, engineers and other professionals are charged with a duty owing to the public whom they serve, it could be said that nothing in the law precludes similar treatment of professional educators. Nor would creation of a standard with which to judge an educator's performance of that duty necessarily pose an insurmountable obstacle. As for proximate causation, while this element might indeed be difficult, if not impossible, to prove in view of the many collateral factors involved in the learning process, it perhaps assumes too much to conclude that it could never be established. This would leave only the element of injury, and who can in good faith deny that a student who upon graduation from high school cannot comprehend simple English—a deficiency allegedly attributable to the negligence of his educators—has not in some fashion been "injured"?[3]

The real issue, the court said, was not whether a cause of action might be cited but whether public policy considerations support the idea of education malpractice suits. The judges unanimously refused to involve the court in the unresolved educational questions that underlie malpractice suits.

What conditions might dispose a court to accept educational malpractice as a legitimate cause of injury?

First, the suit would have to overcome the major public policy objections cited in previous decisions. This would occur more readily if the circumstances of the suit were unique to a single student. Such a case would present a parallel to cases involving professional/client relationships, which the courts regularly consider. Peter W. and Edward Donohue were representative of large numbers of students who fail to acquire basic skills. Their suits raised the specter of myriad similar suits from disgruntled students and an incalculable drain on public funds.

Second, the plaintiff would be able to clearly identify elements of negligence: an obvious breach of an explicit duty, a measurable injury, an undeniable cause-and-effect relationship.

Ironically, a case fitting this description was later reviewed by the same appellate court that had heard the Donohue case. In this case, the appellate court ruled that school authorities had been negligent. However, this decision was soon reversed by New York's highest court for the same policy-related reasons that led the appellate court to reject Donohue's claims.

Daniel Hoffman v. New York Board of Education[4]

Daniel Hoffman was born and raised in the borough of Queens, in New York City. His parents were immigrants. His father died when he was 13 months old, a critical stage of mental and physical development. His mother went to work and his grandmother cared for him.

Shortly before his was five, his mother took him to the National Hospital for Speech Disorders. Hospital records note that Daniel was "a friendly child with little or no intelligible speech." A psychologist found that he had an IQ of 90. The interpretation of the test was that he "could work well into the average and even brighter range. . . . Performance suggests organic dysfunction in speech expressive areas, since he generally appears to understand well and respond as well as able to questions and directions."

Daniel was enrolled in weekly speech therapy seminars.

When Daniel entered kindergarten, he was tested by a school psychologist, found to have an IQ of 74, and placed in a class for children with retarded mental development (CRMD). The psychologist's report stated: "He is not yet able to do formal learning. He needs help with his speech problem in order that he learn to make himself understood. Also, his intelligence should be reevaluated *within a two-year period so that a more accurate estimation of his abilities can be made."*

An IQ score of 75 was the cutoff point for CRMD placement. If Daniel had scored at least 75, he would not have been classified as retarded, and he would not have been placed in classes for the retarded. School authorities made no effort to seek out Daniel's social history. They did not tell his mother that the diagnosis that he was retarded was based on his falling short by one point, nor did they tell her she could request that the IQ test be repeated.

Daniel attended CRMD classes for 11 years without being retested. Teachers who observed his poor performance on achievement tests assumed that his IQ was no better than originally indicated. They apparently did not consider the possibility that his severe speech problem and resulting emotional complications may have masked a higher intelligence.

When he was 18, Daniel's IQ was again tested. This time he was judged to have an IQ of 94. The report noted that he was "so incapacitated by a speech defect that communication is difficult for him." Later testing showed that he had no brain damage.

At the trial, competent witnesses testified that Daniel had a "defective self-image, feelings of inadequacy, diminished incentive, and diminished capacity to learn." Being placed in the CRMD class had resulted in an alteration of Daniel's concept of himself.

School authorities claimed that teachers in the CRMD class were constantly reevaluating Daniel. Teachers testified that Daniel could never have been successful in normal classes.

The court majority, however, ruled that the original report which had placed Daniel in CRMD classes called for retesting his IQ. The court accepted the testimony of the school's own psychiatrist that there was a difference between IQ and achievement. To argue that CRMD teachers were constantly observing students for signs of improvement and reevaluating them was to make meaningless the report's specific request that Daniel's intelligence be reevaluated after two years. If there was any ambiguity about what was required, it was the fault of the school's psychologist who prepared the report and the teachers who failed to seek clarification.

In this case, unlike other educational malpractice suits, the court found a clear duty of care. The school system's "affirmative act in placing plaintiff in CRMD class initially (when it should have known that a mistake could have devastating consequences) created a relationship between itself and plaintiff out of which arose a duty to take reasonable steps to ascertain whether (at least, in a borderline case) that placement was proper."

The Hoffman court concluded that reason, justice, and law supported Daniel's right of recovery. In placing him in a special class on the basis of ambiguous test results that justified a proviso that he be retested, the school system assumed a special duty of care. Although his records called for retesting—and any teacher could have, at any time, and at little expense or inconvenience, ordered an IQ test—Daniel's intelligence was not retested. The retest proviso represented the school system's own standard of care, which it failed to achieve.

The dissenting judges made three points. First, Daniel was constantly observed and evaluated in the CRMD class. Neither his mother nor any experienced teachers ever felt that he was misplaced. His teachers testified that he never performed beyond their expectations and that he could not have functioned in a regular class.

Second, the courts should not oversee or evaluate the professional judgments of those charged with responsibility for the administration of public education. Judges and juries are not equipped to second-guess the appropriateness of tests, placements, or educational programs.

Third, the failure of educational achievement cannot be considered an injury. Education is a benefit conferred on the otherwise ignorant. Daniel was no worse off for having been in the CRMD class. The school may have failed to remedy Daniel's speech problems, but it did not cause or aggravate them.

A five-to-three majority on the Court of Appeals, New York's highest court, reversed the lower-court majority decision. The significant issue, the court said, was whether considerations of public policy preclude recovery for an alleged failure to properly evaluate the intellectual capacity of a student. Daniel's negligence action represented an attack on the professional judgment of the board of education. As the court stated in Donohue v. Copiague, this type of action should not, as a matter of public policy, be entertained by the courts. Educational affairs are vested with the New York State Board of Regents, the state commissioner of education, and local boards of education. The courts should not substitute their judgment for the judgment of educators and government officials actually engaged in the educational process.

Donohue and Peter W. claimed that the schools were negligent in not providing them with a positive program for learning. The schools did not help them attain a reasonable level of reading and writing ability. Essentially, the schools left them alone and allowed them to fail.

In contrast, Hoffman argued that the school system, through positive action, had injured him and destroyed his life chances. The school system had incorrectly placed him in a class for the retarded and failed to identify its error, as it would have had it adhered to its own policies. In the words of Daniel Diamond, a professor at Hofstra University Law School, through "affirmative acts of negligence the school system imposed additional and crippling burdens upon a student."[5]

Unlike the injuries claimed by Donohue and Peter W., Hoffman's injuries were palpable. Although he had normal intelligence, when he graduated from school his personality, perspective, and skills were comparable to those of a retarded person—and he knew it. The lower court noted that by the age of 26, he had not made any advancement in his vocational life nor any particular improvement in his social life. Nobody knows what Daniel Hoffman might have become had he been educated as a normal child or given the speech therapy he needed. What is clear is that he was marked for life by his CRMD experience.

For a short time it looked as though Hoffman would be the opening wedge for educational malpractice suits. Yet it hardly seemed possible that the same court that had slammed the door on such suits in the Donohue decision would open the door so soon thereafter. Perhaps the particulars of the Hoffman case were similar to those envisioned by the majority of the New York Court of Appeals in its Donohue decision, when it acknowledged the possibility of demonstrating educational malpractice. Finally, though, the court declined to substitute its judgment for that of school officials. To do so, the court said, would be to open the door to an examination of the propriety of each of the procedures used in the education of every student. It ruled that the court system is not the proper forum in which to test the validity of educational decisions.

Defamation

Defamation is communication that damages a person's reputation. Defamatory communication holds people up to contempt, causes them to lose the confidence and respect of others, and, consequently, causes them to be shunned or avoided. To prove defamation, one must show that harmful comments were *told to a third party* and *were understood.* It is not necessary to prove malice or ill will, or to demonstrate actual damage.

Defamation may be thought of as a form of malpractice. Defamation may occur when professionals abuse their positions and use their knowledge and power to stain the reputations of clients. Teachers are concerned lest they defame their students. Will their words be used against them if they write honest letters of recommendation? Can they be sued for making written notes of student behavior which they consider odd? Can they be sued for describing the behavior as "strange"? What about calling a student "strange"?

The main reason for such fears seems to be the Buckley Amendment and similar state laws that open students' records to students and parents. Teachers are afraid that recording frank and honest evaluations of students will get them into trouble. And it is a fact that many parents have become skeptical of teachers' abilities to evaluate students.

It is unnecessary to go deeper into the technical definition of defamation because teachers and school administrators have *conditional immunity* against charges of defamation. Conditional immunity ensures that, under certain circumstances, people can't be prosecuted. In the case of a teacher or school administrator, the particular circumstance is the "public interest privilege," which means that statements made by one public official to another public official in pursuit of the public interest are immune to charges of libel.

Public school teachers are public officials. Their public responsibility is to educate and evaluate the performance of students. Teachers are charged with acting in the educational interests of their students, within the limits of their professional competence. If a student is unable to perform in school, it is the responsibility of the teacher and the school to determine why and to help the student. Additionally, it is the teacher's responsibility to prevent one student from harming the rest of the students. Conditional immunity protects reasonable communications that are made for these purposes.

The word "conditional" indicates that there are limits to what an educator can say and do. To qualify as privileged, a communication must be made *in a reasonable manner* and *for a proper purpose.*

What these phrases mean is that a teacher may discuss a student and a student's problems with colleagues and supervisors as long as the teacher believes that such discussions are in the student's interest and/or in the public interest. The teacher loses this privilege if the communication is made for any purpose that is not considered "proper." The teacher must not be motivated by malice or by desire to harm the student.

In these days of specialization, it is important to remember that teachers' comments must reflect their areas of competence. Few teachers are also trained as psychologists, psychiatrists, social workers, or medical doctors. It is inappropriate for a teacher who is not trained in such a specialty to adopt its jargon or techniques in attempting to diagnose a student's problems.When a teacher observes that a student's work is not up to expectations, the appropriate response is to consult a supervisor and refer the student to an appropriate specialist.

The chances that a responsible teacher will ever have to go to court to defend against a charge of defamation are nil. Although laws providing for full disclosure may have increased teachers' anxiety, they have not affected teachers' liability. What these laws have done is ensure that legitimate evaluations of students will be accessible to parents. Making such evaluations has always been consistent with a teacher's public-interest privilege. If greater accessibility of student evaluations encourages greater sensitivity to the limits of conditional immunity, everyone will benefit.

To illustrate the unlikelihood that an educator will be sued for defamation, it is necessary to go back to 1920 to find an example.

Baskett v. Crossfield[6]
Dr. Crossfield was the president of Transylvania University, a coeducational institution in Lexington, Kentucky. Oscar Baskett was a student who had been expelled. Baskett's father sued the university president for explaining to him, in a personal letter, the reasons for young Baskett's expulsion. He claimed that this "public record" had defamed his son.

What had Crossfield's letter said? He had reported to Mr. Baskett that Oscar had been expelled for exposing himself indecently from his dormitory window. People on the road and sidewalk below had seen him.

The court sided with Crossfield. They ruled that his letter was not a "public record" but a privileged communica-

> tion—one made *"in good faith without malice, and volun-*
> *tarily, but . . . in performance of a duty to society in the*
> *belief that the communication is true." Further, the court*
> said, *"Where a party makes a communication prompted by a*
> *duty owed either to the public or to a third person . . . the*
> *communication is privileged if made in good faith and*
> *without actual malice."*

More recently, in *Meyers v. Chicago Board of Education,* the Illinois Court of Appeals rejected a suit brought by a school employee over a statement that the director of civil service personnel had made about him. The court ruled, "Where the director of civil service personnel was acting as [the board's] duly authorized agent and was employed within the scope of his employment, the board was immune from liability for the director's alleged slanderous statement concerning an employee of the board."[7] A similar rule applies to teachers when they are *acting as agents of the school system and performing within the scope of their employment.*

Some state legislatures have sought to give teachers added assurance that their right to candidly evaluate students will be protected. For example, Maryland's legislature has adopted a statute providing that "a teacher, guidance counselor or member of an administrative or educational staff of any public, private or parochial school is immune from civil liability for (1) making a report required by law, if he acts on reasonable grounds, and (2) participating in a judicial proceeding that results from his report."[8]

All teachers are protected by the conditional immunity afforded by common-law public-interest privileges. In some states, teachers have specific additional statutory protection. Two additional points should be noted: First, in most states truth is a recognized defense.[9] (Truth, however, should not be used as a shield for malevolence.) Good motives, justifiable ends, and the need to make honest evaluations offer protection against defamation actions in all states. Second, in the event of an honest mistake, a timely retraction may lead to dismissal of a defamation suit. The courts usually accept a timely retraction or correction as evidence of worthy intention.

Malpractice and defamation suits are headline-grabbing scare words. They do not constitute realistic threats to educators.

If it is unreasonable for teachers to fear educational malpractice and defamation suits, why is there so much publicity about them? The rarity of such actions accounts in large part for the disproportionate attention they receive in the news media.

Of course, educators must exercise professional responsibility, but worrying about malpractice or defamation suits is a waste of energy. Efforts to understand the law will be much more rewarding.

Notes to Chapter 4

1. *Peter W. v. San Francisco United School District,* 131 Cal. Rptr. 854 (App., 1976).

2. *Edward Donohue v. Copiague Union School District,* 408 N.Y.S. 2d 584 (Supreme Ct., 1977); affirmed, 407 N.Y.S. 2d 874 (A.D., 1978); affirmed, 418 (N.Y.S. 2d 375 (Ct. of App., 1979).

3. Ibid. at 377.

4. *Daniel Hoffman v. New York Board of Education,* 410 N.Y.S. 2d 99 (A.D., 1978); reversed, 424 N.Y.S. 2d 376 (Ct. of App., 1979).

5. D. Diamond, "Education Law," 29 *Syracuse Law Review* 107, pp. 150-151.

6. Baskett v. Crossfield, 228 S.W. 673 (Ky. App., 1920).

7. *Meyers v. Chicago Board of Education,* 257 N.E. 2d 183 (Ill. App., 1970). See also *Iverson v. Frandsen,* 237 F. 2d 898 (10th Cir., 1956).

8. *Maryland Education Code Annotated,* Sec. 6-109.

9. W. Prosser, *Handbook of the Law of Facts,* 4th ed. (St. Paul: West Publishing Co., 1974), Sec. 111.

5.

DISCIPLINE

"There is no discipline in schools today. Teachers are helpless; students are out of control." These assertions are components of the mythology that surrounds the issue of student discipline in American schools. Such myths have led many teachers and school officials to believe—incorrectly—that they lack sufficient authority to impose discipline and order.

Few teachers receive, as part of their formal training, much information about the laws that affect their teaching. When, in the 1970s, teachers were confronted by the articulate assertion of student rights, many were overwhelmed. They had taken their own power for granted without knowing the legal basis of their power. Many felt helpless to deal with students who misbehaved or who defied reasonable requests. Often, school administrators—similarly hampered by ignorance and feelings of helplessness—failed to support teachers' disciplinary efforts.

The purpose of this chapter is to spell out the disciplinary authority of teachers. What are the rights and responsibilities of teachers when students misbehave, violate legitimate school rules, or refuse to obey reasonable requests?

Teachers may exercise significant disciplinary authority over students, and they can legitimately insist that school officials support them in exercising their authority. The legal basis of school disciplinary authority is located in both common and statutory law. There is no question that students have significant constitutional rights to due process and First Amendment freedoms. Nevertheless, these rights are balanced against the need of a school to maintain an orderly learning environment. The courts have consistently asserted their support for the efforts of school officials to maintain order. School authorities may write and enforce rules for student behavior, and they may punish students who violate rules. Furthermore, teachers and school administrators may respond immediately when students threaten to harm themselves, others, or school property.

The common-law basis of teacher authority. The common law is the primary source of teacher authority. Teachers have authority to act *in loco parentis*—in place of the parent—to enforce discipline in the school.

In the early days of education, when schooling was a voluntary arrangement, it was understood that the parent gave the teacher the right to discipline the child. This assumption changed when education became compulsory. Today, the courts recognize that it is the state which gives a teacher the implicit right to discipline a child at school as a parent would at home. The parent is powerless to restrict the common-law disciplinary authority of the teacher over the pupil except as provided by statute.

The U.S. Supreme Court acknowledged this important source of teacher authority in its *Ingraham v. Wright* corporal-punishment decision:

> At common law, a single principle has governed the use of corporal punishment since before the American Revolution: teachers may impose reasonable but not excessive force to discipline a child. . . . The basic doctrine has not changed. The prevalent rule in this country today privileges such force as a teacher or administrator "reasonably believes to be necessary for the child's proper control, training, or education."
>
> The view today is "that the State itself may impose such corporal punishment as is reasonably necessary 'for the proper education of the child and for the maintenance of group discipline.'"[1]

Most people think that corporal punishment represents the most extreme disciplinary power available to the teacher. Therefore, common-law authority to impose corporal punishment implies power to impose lesser punishments.

The statutory basis of teacher authority. Statutes in many states buttress the common-law disciplinary authority of school officials. South Carolina school boards are authorized to "promulgate rules prescribing standards of conduct" for pupils.[2] Illinois school boards are authorized to suspend students for gross disobedience or misconduct.[3] Teachers are given explicit *in loco parentis* status in all matters relating to discipline. A Colorado statute lists the types of misbehavior that may lead to suspension, including continued willful disobedience, persistent defiance of proper authority, willful destruction of school property, and behavior that is inimical to the welfare, safety, or morals of other pupils.[4]

Under Connecticut statutes, a board of education may authorize a teacher to remove a pupil from class when such pupil causes a serious disruption of the educational process and may authorize school administrators to suspend any pupil whose conduct endangers persons or property, is seriously disruptive, or violates a publicized school-board policy.[5]

A Georgia statute provides that any principal or teacher, if authorized to do so by policies of the local school board, may administer corporal punishment in order to maintain proper control and discipline over pupils. The statute goes on to delineate a number of safeguards designed to protect pupils from excessive or improper punishment.[6]

A Florida statute makes it a misdemeanor to willfully interrupt or disturb "any school or any assembly of people met for the worship of God or for any lawful purpose." Recently, a junior high school student who had disrupted the school by running down the halls and shouting obscenities at a teacher was successfully prosecuted under this law.[7]

These grants of authority regularly extend to all school-related activities. Some states have made this explicit. An Arkansas statute says: "Any school board in this state shall hold its pupils strictly accountable for any disorderly conduct in school, on the school grounds, in a school bus, or at any school function."[8] Similarly, Illinois law extends the *in-loco-parentis* authority of teachers and school administrators to supervision of extracurricular activities and school transportation.[9] Florida appears to give school bus drivers *in-loco-parentis* power for the limited purpose of maintaining order on school buses.[10]

The Courts and Discipline

How do the courts interpret such laws? Many school people feel that the courts are looking over their shoulders, eagerly awaiting opportunities to reverse disciplinary decisions and undermine the school's authority. This is not the case. When it comes to discipline, the schools get a great deal of support from the courts.

Generally, the courts prefer to stay out of school disputes. In 1968 the Supreme Court noted, in *Epperson v. Arkansas:*

> Judicial interposition in the operation of the public school system of the nation raises problems requiring care and restraint. . . . By and large, public education in our nation is committed to the control of state and local authorities. Courts do not and cannot intervene in the resolution of conflicts which arise in the daily operation of school systems and which do not directly and sharply implicate basic constitutional values.[11]

Supreme Court Justice Stevens made a similar point in a decision he wrote in a 1974 U.S. Court of Appeals case involving hair and dress standards:

> We will not review a school board decision that involves nothing more than a difference of opinion on the question of style. Sometimes such a school board determination will be incorrect. [However], we are persuaded that the importance of allowing school boards sufficient latitude to discharge their responsibilities effectively—and inevitably, therefore, to make mistakes from time to time—outweighs the individual interest at stake.[12]

In 1975 the Supreme Court firmly restated the real limits on federal court intervention in school disciplinary decisions:

> It is not the role of the federal courts to set aside decisions of school administrators which the court may view as lacking a basis in wisdom or compassion. Public high school students do have substantive and procedural rights while at school. [But they do not have] the right to relitigate in federal court evidentiary questions arising in school disciplinary proceedings or the proper construction of school regulations. The system of public education that has evolved in this nation relies necessarily upon the discretion and judgment of school administrators and school board members, and [their actions are not reviewable if they] do not arise to the level of violations of specific constitutional guarantees.[13]

Due Process for Students

The law is written to support the authority of the teacher and the school. Common-law *in-loco-parentis* status gives the teacher a broad range of power. Nevertheless, all grants of authority have limits. The legitimate need of the school to maintain order must be balanced against the students' constitutional guarantees to freedom of speech, press, petition, and assembly. And students may not be punished or deprived of educational benefits without due process.

Courts will intervene in student disciplinary decisions to affirm basic constitutional safeguards. In practice, this means intervention to support students' First Amendment rights in regard to speech, press, and assembly; Fourth Amendment right to be free from unreasonable search; and Fourteenth Amendment right to due process in cases involving suspension or expulsion. The two major precedents are *Tinker v. Board*[14] and *Goss v. Lopez.*[15] In the Tinker decision, the Supreme Court affirmed students' right to free speech when it reversed the suspension of a pupil who had worn an armband to protest U.S. bombing of Vietnam. In the Goss case, the court questioned the fairness of suspending a student without a proper hearing. (A student who had demonstrated at a high school which she did not attend received a telephone call the next morning and was told not to report to school for ten days.)

Due process, in the context of the school, involves two sets of responsibilities. First, school rules must clearly specify the types of misconduct for which students will be punished.[16] Second, school authorities must use fair procedures in determining guilt and punishment.[17]

In most states, schools receive a broad grant of disciplinary power which is couched in very general language. The laws cite such terms as *disobedience, misconduct, disruption, discipline, order,* and *conduct.* In these states it is essential that school authorities develop codes of conduct which specify the meanings of such terms, elaborating the conditions and contexts. It is not sufficient for a school system simply to adopt these terms and invoke them against students in an ad hoc fashion. Rather, *disobedience* must be explicitly defined as "refusal to comply with a reasonable request of the classroom teacher" and *misconduct* as "intentional destruction of school property" or "fighting on school grounds."

For rules to be legitimate, they must emanate from a legitimate authority. The school board is the legitimate authority in a school district, and it should be the source of codes of student conduct. In practice, it is common for school boards to pass on some rule-making authority to school building administrators. Many state codes permit superintendents, principals, or deans to impose short suspensions, a policy which suggests that these officials share legitimate rule-making authority. Nevertheless, the dispersal of rule-making authority almost always leads to confusion and questions about the legitimacy of the rules.[18]

School authorities should give students advance notice of the rules and specify the punishments that may be assigned for various infractions. It is usually considered "sufficient notice" to publish the rules in a handbook and distribute it to students. A Florida statute requires officials of each school to develop a code of student conduct based on the school's rules for student discipline. The code must include the following information: (1) specific grounds for disciplinary action; (2) procedures to be followed for acts requiring discipline, including corporal punishment; and (3) an explanation of the responsibilities and rights of students with regard to attendance, respect for persons and property, knowledge and observation of rules of conduct, the right to learn, free speech and student publications, assembly, privacy, and participation in school programs and activities.[19]

While it is necessary to have specific rules, the school code need not anticipate all eventualities and types of misconduct. The courts recognize that some behavior is grossly out of line by any standard. In many cases, students are expected to have been able to anticipate that their conduct would be unacceptable.

Supreme Court Justice Blackmun made this point in a 1970 lower-court decision concerning a college student who had been expelled for misconduct.[20] Blackmun pointed out that there were clearly defined standards of acceptable behavior, of which everyone of college age should be aware—among them, decency, nonviolence, respect for the rights of others, and respect for property. He concluded that some rules of conduct do not have to be specifically stated. Less-mature students, however, probably require more-explicit guidelines.

The second requirement of due process is adherence to a series of procedural steps which can prevent error or excess. Every minor child has the right to an education. Courts have accepted educators at their word when they insist that every day of school is important. Therefore, school authorities must safeguard against inappropriately depriving students of the right to an education.

Courts are fond of saying that due process is flexible. Often, the question before the court is: What process is due? Simply stated, due process calls for procedural protections appropriate to meet particular situations. The need for safeguards increases with the severity of the potential punishment. In the Goss decision, the Supreme Court held that due process requires a student facing a short suspension (fewer than ten days) to be charged with specific misconduct.[21] If the student denies the charges, school authorities must present their evidence and give the student an opportunity to appeal the decision. Such lesser punishments as corporal punishment and detention, because they do not deprive students of an education, require less in the way of procedural safeguards. Severe punishments—for example, expulsion—require the full panoply of due-process protection.

Disciplinary Options

What types of disciplinary measures are available to teachers and schools? The courts have supported the following types of restrictions and punishments: (1) criticism of students, (2) detention and in-school suspension, (3) corporal punishment, (4) physical control or restraint, (5) grade reduction, (6) suspension from extracurricular activity, (7) suspension from school, (8) transfer, and (9) expulsion. In addition, the courts have recognized that the need to maintain order and safety in the schools may justify the search of students' lockers and, under some circumstances, their persons.

Because due process is a flexible concept, each disciplinary act calls forth its own measure of due process. Because minor disciplinary actions do not implicate constitutional issues, courts tend to stay clear of them. But what is "minor"?

In *Linwood v. Peoria Board of Education,* the U.S. Court of Appeals noted: "Certainly, the imposition of disciplinary measures such as after-school detention, restriction to the classroom during free periods, reprimand, or admonition does not *per se* involve matter rising to the dignity of constitutional magnitude."[22] Minor punishments are those that do not threaten to deprive a student of an education. These punishments seldom become cases for the courts.

Courts have generally upheld such minor punishments as verbal criticism, detention, and in-school suspension.

Criticism of Students

The courts have supported the authority of teachers to criticize their students and to send them into a hall or detention room.[23] When teacher Juanita Scott was challenged for calling a fifth-grade pupil "worthless, undependable, and incompetent," an Illinois Appeals Court ruled that, acting *in loco parentis,* she had the authority to do so. The court ruled, "In the absence of malice or wantonness, it may well be that disparaging comments about a pupil may be necessary and perhaps conducive to proper educational discipline."[24]

Detention and In-School Suspension

In what appears to be the only case ever heard dealing with after-school detention, the Supreme Court of Indiana declared the practice benign. The court wrote:

> The detention . . . of pupils for a short time after the rest of the class have been dismissed . . . has been very generally adopted by the schools . . . and it is now one of the recognized methods of enforcing discipline, and promoting the progressive of pupils. . . . It is a mild and nonaggressive method of imposing a penalty and inflicts no disgrace upon the pupil.[25]

In the 1970s, in-school suspension became a popular alternative to suspension or expulsion. School officials allowed students to remain in the school but took away normal opportunities for physical mobility and social interaction. Often they assigned the students to a single room, sometimes called the jail or cell, and did not permit them to speak. Under the watchful eyes of an instructor, the students were encouraged to complete assigned lessons. Thus, in-school suspension satisfied the goals of both discipline and education.

In-school suspension falls within the authority of the school to assign students to programs or classes. It raises no constitutional issues because the student remains in school and is not deprived of any educational benefits. This perspective was endorsed by a U.S. District Court sitting in Pennsylvania. The court described the punishment:

He was ordered to report to a room which his lawyer calls a "jail room," supervised by a teacher and required to do his assigned school work, which, near the end of the school year, would seem a most appropriate time for review. His 11-day in-school restriction did not deprive him of any in-school education. Since he graduated at the conclusion of the 11-day restriction, it seems apparent that he did not receive any material educational injury.[26]

The student in this case also missed a one-day senior class trip to Philadelphia because of his suspension. The court said, "Participation in a sightseeing trip is not a constitutionally protected right."[27]

Corporal Punishment

Although corporal punishment has been the subject of a great many laws and court decisions, it does not raise any constitutional issues. As noted earlier, in 1977 the U.S. Supreme Court upheld the constitutionality of corporal punishment. In addition, the majority rejected the need for due process, saying the case for safeguards was not compelling. The court said:

We have found frequently that some kind of prior hearing is necessary to guard against arbitrary impositions on interests protected by the Fourteenth Amendment.

In view of the low incidence of abuse, the openness of our schools, and the common-law safeguards that already exist, the risk of error that may result in violation of a school child's substantive rights . . . [is] minimal. [Such] safeguards . . . might reduce the risk marginally, but would also entail a significant intrusion into an area of primary educational responsibility. We conclude that the Due Process Clause does not require notice and a hearing prior to the imposition of corporal punishment.[28]

The court simply saw no need to make a federal case out of corporal punishment; instead, it would rely on individual states to deal with instances of excessive or unjustified corporal punishment.

It is necessary and useful to distinguish corporal punishment from the action of striking a student. Corporal punishment is a deliberate process.[29] State statutes and school regulations often establish the following prerequisites for corporal punishment: warning notice, statement of reasons, opportunity for the student to explain his or her side, cooling-off period, use of a paddle or other prescribed instrument on the buttocks, administration of the punishment in private, presence of a second teacher or administrator to act as a witness. Striking a student to demand attention, to reassert authority, or in the heat of an argument should not be confused with corporal punishment.[30]

Some states have adopted elaborate statutes to regulate the use of corporal punishment. Georgia is a prime example:

- The corporal punishment shall not be excessive or unduly severe.
- Corporal punishment shall never be used as a first line of punishment for misbehavior unless the pupil was informed beforehand that specific misbehavior could occasion its use; provided, however, that corporal punishment may be employed as a first line of punishment for those acts of misconduct which are so antisocial or disruptive in nature as to shock the conscience.
- Corporal punishment must be administered in the presence of a principal or [other designated school administrator, who] must be informed beforehand and in the presence of the pupil of the reason for the punishment.
- The principal or teacher who administered corporal punishment must provide the child's parent, upon request, a written explanation of the reasons for the punishment. Provided however that such an explanation shall not be used as evidence in any subsequent civil action brought as a result of said corporal punishment.
- Corporal punishment shall not be administered to a child whose parents or legal guardian have upon the day of enrollment of the pupil filed with the principal of the school a statement from a medical doctor licensed in Georgia stating that it is detrimental to the child's mental or emotional stability.[31]

Physical Restraint

Corporal punishment is only one kind of physical coercion available to teachers. Teachers are also authorized to physically control or restrain students when they threaten to harm themselves or others or when they refuse to obey legitimate requests. Two court decisions illustrate this power of the teacher:

Simms v. School District[32]

An eighth-grade student, Richard Simms, persisted in talking instead of working on his assignment. The teacher told him to leave the room. Simms responded, "I don't have to do what this m----- f----- says."

The teacher left his desk, took the student by the arm, and tried to eject him physically. The student resisted, kicked, flayed, and pulled away; he then swung his arm and cut it on a window.

The question, the Oregon appeals court said, is: Can a teacher use reasonable force to remove a disruptive child from a classroom? The answer is: Yes. The teacher stands in loco parentis *and thus shares the parent's right to obtain obedience to reasonable commands by force. Oregon statutes call on pupils to submit to the teacher's authority. Willful disobedience, open defiance of a teacher's authority, or the use of profane language is sufficient cause for punishment, suspension, or expulsion from school.*

Andreozzi v. Rubano[33]
Louis Rubano, a junior high school teacher in New Haven, Connecticut, was in charge of the detention room. Dom Andreozzi, a student, was creating a disturbance. Rubano took the student's arm to escort him from the room, but he pulled away and became loud and profane. When they reached the hall, the student clenched his fists and assumed a belligerent attitude. Rubano struck the student across the face.

The judge began by saying that the teacher stands in-loco-parentis toward the pupil. The school's rule that only the principal can administer corporal punishment was not relevant. Rubano acted, not for the purpose of inflicting punishment, but to restore order and discipline. If he had not taken prompt and effective action in response to the sudden and violent outburst, he would have been humiliated in the eyes of his pupils, and order and discipline would have suffered.

Although the power to restrain students falls within the common-law authority of the schools, some states have seen fit to codify this power in statutes. For example, Connecticut law states: "Any . . . board of education may authorize teachers . . . to remove a pupil from class when such pupil deliberately causes serious disruption. . . ."[34]

Grade Reduction

Grade reduction is a traditional disciplinary tool available to most teachers. In recent years, however, there has been a significant movement away from this use of grading. Grades which purport to measure a student's academic performance and progress are misleading when they are also used as punishment for misbehavior. At least one state appeals court has recognized that disciplinary grade reductions represent a significant potential for educational deprivation.

In a series of decisions, the New Jersey commissioner of education disallowed the use of grades to punish students.[35] The commissioner reasoned that absence because of truancy or suspension would inevitably affect a student's grades because of lost class time; the student should not be additionally penalized. Such a student should be allowed to make up work and take objective exams. Assigning zeros for missed work and allowing the term grade to be weighted down by the zeros, the commissioner ruled, is improper. A California statute specifically provides that a suspended pupil shall be allowed to make up missed assignments and tests and "shall be given full credit therefor."[36]

Two Illinois appeals courts have dealt with the issue of reducing student grades as punishment. In the first case, the court upheld the practice of lowering a student's grade as punishment for truancy.[37] In response to orders from the principal, three teachers reduced a student's quarter grades by one letter. The court said that the punishment was not so harsh as to deprive the student of substantive due process. Since the decision came significantly later than the event, the court was able to note that there was no evidence that the student had been harmed by the punishment.

A second, more-recent decision raised a series of questions about grade reduction policies:

Hamer v. Board of Education[38]

Eli Hamer, a high school student, left school during the lunch period. She cut three classes without notifying any teacher or staff member. On the next school day she was told that her punishment would be a 3-percent reduction in the grades of the courses she cut. The high school principal had developed the policy under a grant of authority from the school board.

In court, Hamer argued that she had been deprived of due process. First, the punishment was not authorized by either a school board regulation or state statute. Second, the policy was enforced differently depending on the school, the department, and the teacher. Third, the grade reduction lowered her overall average.

The court said that the case raised several serious ques-

tions: Was the policy authorized by the board? Was Hamer given a chance to explain her actions before the principal imposed the punishment? Was application of the policy arbitrary and capricious? The case was returned to the lower court to determine if the procedures for developing and enforcing the policy were consistent with due process and whether the grade reduction had a reasonable relationship to disciplinary objectives sought by the school board.

Grade reduction as a disciplinary measure can constitute a serious deprivation, especially in a high competitive academic environment. Athough most teachers and school officials believe that they have the authority to punish students this way, the practice has come under increasing scrutiny. The Illinois appeals court in *Hamer* did not disallow the use of grades for disciplinary purposes, but it raised important due-process concerns that affect the rights and responsibilities of teachers.

Denial of Extracurricular Participation

For many years, educators have debated the role of extracurricular activities in the school program. Are they important? Are they essential? Although such questions remain for the most part unanswered, extracurricular activities are clearly part of the traditional package of opportunities offered to students, and the courts have ruled that the right to take advantage of these opportunities deserves some protection.

However, courts have given schools some latitude in using withdrawal of the right to participate in extracurricular activities as a means of punishing misbehavior. In *Hasson v. Boothby,* U.S. District Court Judge Garrity permitted three students to be placed on probation and excluded from school athletic teams for drinking beer off-campus before a school dance.[39] And in *Zeller v. Donegal,* the court refused to intervene when a student was expelled from the soccer team because his hair was too long.[40]

Braesch v. DePasquale[41]
The rules of conduct for members of the boys' and girls' basketball teams of Arlington High read: "Drinking, smoking, or drugs—Do not come out for basketball if you plan on using any of the above. Any use of them will result in immediate expulsion from the squad."
One Saturday night several team members attended a party at which they consumed alcoholic beverages. When the

coaches learned of the party, they questioned the students. The students admitted breaking the rules, and they were expelled from the teams.

On review, the Nebraska Supreme Court upheld the authority of the school to make and enforce their disciplinary policies.

The court began its decision by noting that there is disagreement whether participation in school athletics is a constitutional right. A student's interest in athletic participation is clearly less important than participation in academic education. Nevertheless, the student's interest is significant, and the question becomes: What protection is necessary to ensure that a student is not unduly deprived of a property or liberty interest?

The students, the court concluded, had received due process because (1) they knew the rules; (2) thus the students had admitted breaking the rules, no hearing was required to establish guilt—in any case, the students and their parents had met with the principal and been offered a hearing before the board; and (3) the rule was a reasonable means to a valid educational objective: deterring student athletes from using alcohol.

Suspension and Expulsion

Although classroom teachers ordinarily are not directly involved with student suspensions and expulsions, these options are important adjuncts to the teacher's disciplinary authority. Court decisions and statutory changes have led to confusion about the availability of these disciplinary options, especially in regard to due-process requirements, which has made some school officials unduly hesitant to employ these options. Therefore, it is essential for teachers to understand that suspension and expulsion remain acceptable disciplinary alternatives for school officials.

In *Goss v. Lopez,* the Supreme Court ruled that before suspending a student for up to ten days, the school must provide the student with a hearing.[42] The hearing can be informal and need last no longer than five minutes. During this hearing, the student must be told what he or she is accused of. If the student denies the accusation, the school must present its evidence or witnesses and listen to the student's explanation. Students who are threatened with short suspensions have no right to a lawyer or other representative, no right to cross-examine witnesses, nor any other right associated with due-process hearings. Only the rudiments of fairness are required.

Longer suspensions and expulsions call for more-elaborate due-process safeguards. Those procedures which need to be followed to ensure a fair result should be identified by school officials and school board members with the help of competent legal counsel.

Gonzales v. McEuen[43]

Students rioted at Oxnard High School. Steve Gonzales and ten other students were charged with a number of joint and separate acts which led to the riot. The Board of Trustees conducted hearings, sustained the charges, and expelled the students. The students claimed that their due-process rights had been violated.

Based on the facts of the particular case, the federal district court said that students faced with expulsion had the following rights:

- *Notice of a hearing should include (1) a statement of specific charges and (2) a list of the student's basic hearing rights, including the right to be present and the rights to counsel, to present evidence, and to cross-examine witnesses.*
- *Evidence must be more than hearsay. Witnesses should be under oath and available for cross-examination by the students.*
- *A student's right against self-incrimination is violated if prosecuting counsel comments on the student's refusal to testify.*
- *An impartial hearing requires that those who prosecute the case not also act as counsel to members of the hearing tribunal. The presence of the superintendent at the hearing may inhibit the board and introduce bias.*
- *The decision must be based on competent credible evidence.*

The court sustained some of the expulsions and reversed others, depending on the particular circumstances of each student's expulsion.

Although federal courts require a minimal due-process hearing for suspensions of less than ten days, state laws and department of education regulations may require more-elaborate procedures for shorter suspensions. Maryland law permits principals to suspend students for cause for five days and requires a parental conference during the suspension.[44] County superintendents are required to investigate requests for longer suspensions, and suspensions of more than ten days call for a full hearing.

In New Hampshire, parents can appeal six-day suspensions to

the school board, and the board must approve suspensions of longer than twenty days.[45] In Wisconsin, a student cannot be suspended for more than three school days unless the school begins an expulsion procedure.[46] Students and parents are entitled to appeal the decision before an impartial representative of the school system.

Search and Seizure

The U.S. Supreme Court has ruled that "searches conducted outside the judicial process without prior approval by judge or magistrate are *per se* unreasonable."[47] School officials should consider obtaining a search warrant before they search a student. This is a sound and constitutional strategy for nonemergency situations.

Generally, the courts agree that the standard for justifying a warrantless search is less rigorous for a school official than for the police.[48] School officials are not concerned with the discovery and prevention of crime. Their primary duty is to maintain order and discipline in the school. To do so often requires taking immediate action. It would be an unreasonable burden to hold school officials to a police standard of "probable cause" and require them to obtain search warrants. Many courts have held that school officials may search a student if they have *reasonable cause to believe that the search is necessary to the maintenance of order and discipline.*

If school officials step outside their *in-loco-parentis* role and act as police would to seek out evidence of crime, the courts may insist that they conform to the higher standards of "probable cause" required for police searches. School officials lose their protected parental status when they work hand in glove with police. Failure to conform to the higher standard may subject school officials to civil rights suits in federal courts.[49]

Courts have generally upheld warrantless locker searches.[50] School lockers are public property merely loaned to students. The student is given the use of the locker for certain limited purposes. The need to protect school property and students should be adequate to justify a locker search.

When considering the legality of a search, the court will often ask whether the person had a reasonable expectation of privacy. Thus, courts have upheld the visual inspection of the interior of a locked car but have voided convictions based on inspections of closed car trunks, suitcases, or houses. Recently, the Supreme Court ruled that a paper bag did not offer a reasonable expectation of privacy.[51] Given the circumstances under which students are assigned lockers, it seems likely that courts will rule that school lockers do not offer a reasonable expectation of privacy.

A search of a student's person or personal property is an entirely different matter. School officials have the authority to maintain discipline and order in the schools. They must protect the students and school property. The students have a Fourth Amendment right to be free from unreasonable search and seizure. What is "unreasonable"? The reasonableness of a search depends on the circumstances. Courts consider the following factors in deciding whether a particular search is reasonable:

• *The student's age, record, and disciplinary history.* A student with a history of misconduct and disciplinary problems is a more reasonable subject for a search than a student with a good record.

• *The prevalence and seriousness of the problem which motivates the search.* A continuing problem with drugs or weapons in the school might justify a search for contraband; a harmless prank probably would not.

• *The need for swift action in making the search.* An imminent danger justifies immediate action. If there is no danger and no likelihood that the contraband will disappear, school officials should seek a search warrant.

• *The reliability of the information used to justify the search.* School authorities must have reasonable grounds to believe that such information is accurate.

• *The extent to which the search intrudes on the privacy of the student.* A "pat-down" is more intrusive than a request that a student account for bulges in his pockets. A strip search is more intrusive than a search of a student's pockets. The more intrusive the search, the greater the violation of the student's privacy and the greater the need for prior justification.[52]

Picha v. Wielgos[53]

A school principal, Raymond Wielgos, received a phone call which led him to suspect that Renee Picha, a 13-year-old pupil, possessed illegal drugs. He called the police. When the police arrived, Renee was strip-searched by the school nurse.

The court said that the disciplinary and educational concerns of school officials give them some latitude in dealing with the civil rights of students. However, in this case, the

*police were immediately involved and the search was a quest
for illegal items. "Where the police have significant participation, Fourth Amendment rights cannot leak out the hole of
presumed consent to a search by an ordinarily nongovern-
mental party. . . . The standard . . . becomes either probable
cause, or else whether the quasi-governmental party could
reasonably perform the search in the exercise of his official
responsibilities."*

*The court ruled that, although the school has an interest
in the safety of students, all it can do is locate and perhaps
confiscate the drugs: "In loco parentis cannot vitiate the
constitutional expectation of privacy which creates the need
for levels of suspicion or exigency in the conduct of a criminal
investigation."*

So it is up to school authorities to make an early determination
of whether they are dealing with a school problem or a criminal
problem. If it is a criminal problem, they should turn the case over
to the police and withdraw. However, as surrogate parents, it would
not be unfitting for school officials to counsel students on their
rights.[54]

Bellnier v. Lund[55]

*A student told his teacher that $3.00 was missing from
his coat pocket. The coat had been hanging in the rear of the
fifth-grade classroom. When no student would confess to the
theft, teachers searched the coats of all the students. Finding
nothing, the teachers had the students empty their pockets
and remove their shoes. Again finding nothing, the teachers
took the students to the restrooms and had them strip to their
underwear.*

*The court said that the teachers were acting under the
color of state authority and that the students had a Fourth
Amendment right to be free from unreasonable searches.
Students have a right to privacy, and they need to be protected from the humiliation and the psychological harm that
a search may cause. School officials, however, must maintain
a safe atmosphere and proper discipline. Thus, while school
officials are not held to the same standard of "probable
cause" that is required of police, they must be able to demonstrate that they had reasonable grounds to search a student
and that the search served a legitimate school purpose.*

*In this case, the school officials may have had reason-
able suspicion or even probable cause to believe that someone
in the class possessed the stolen money. However, they had
no reason to suspect that each student who was searched*

> *possessed evidence of a crime. Given the very slight danger involved, the extensiveness of the search, and the tender age of the students, the search was not reasonable.*

The Long Reach of the School

The physical and emotional well-being of students may be affected not only by what occurs within the confines of a school but also by events outside school. Physical violence, threats to school property, or delinquent behavior, wherever they occur, can threaten the discipline and general welfare of a school. Recognizing this, the courts permit schools to exercise disciplinary authority over students even when certain kinds of offensive behavior take place off campus and independent of school functions.

The general rule is that school authorities can discipline pupils for out-of-school conduct which has a direct and immediate effect on the welfare of the school and students.[56] This is positively the case when the purpose of disciplinary action is not to punish a student but rather to protect the school community from the adverse influence of the offender. However, schools may also regulate some off-campus activities which educators perceive as being harmful to students' welfare.

Generally, school personnel should not interfere in the private lives of students. School authorities are on shaky ground if they try to regulate student behavior that has no immediate effect on the school or on other students. Nevertheless, the courts have permitted some interference. As we saw in the Braesch case, the Nebraska Supreme Court upheld disciplinary action against athletic team members who broke training rules. The no-drinking rule was clearly designed to protect the students' welfare and not to protect the school from bad influences. It seems unlikely, however, that the court would have upheld punishment more extreme than suspension from the team.

School authorities are on firmer ground when a student's off-campus action presents a direct threat to other students. Such a threat was clearly identifiable in a case recently decided by the Wyoming Supreme Court.[57] In this case, a student drove past a school bus at a stop sign and proceeded at a speed far below the limit. When the bus driver tried to pass the student's jeep, the student speeded up and prevented the bus from passing. The court held that school authorities could justifiably discipline the student because the purpose of the punishment was to protect other students from a potentially unsafe situation.

The courts have accepted the proposition that drug-related offenses represent a potential danger to the school community.[58] Many state legislatures have adopted statutes which expressly identify drug-related offenses as grounds for suspension from school.[59] Cooperation with authorities can mitigate the punishment.

The school environment is sensitive to disruption as well as danger. Courts have been sympathetic to school officials when off-campus student behavior threatens their authority and their ability to control the school.

Fenton v. Stear[60]

Students at Merion Center High School in Pennsylvania were sitting in a car. It was a Sunday, and they were parked at a shopping mall several miles from school. A teacher drove by and one student, Jeff Fenton, yelled out, "He's a p----!"

At school the next day, the vice-principal confronted Fenton with the facts of the incident and he admitted his indiscretion. Fenton was placed on immediate in-school suspension for three days and forbidden to participate in a class trip planned for the following day.

The U.S. District Court upheld the action of the school authorities. There is no right to vulgar speech. The incident was a matter for discipline within the discretion of school authorities. Due process was satisfied when the student admitted the accusation. The punishment did not deprive the student of his right to an education. To countenance such student conduct without imposing sanctions could lead to devastating consequences in the school.

Parents and teachers consistently identify student discipline as a major problem confronting the schools. This is not for want of sufficient legal authority and disciplinary options. State legislatures and courts have supported the efforts of school people to create an orderly learning environment. Despite this support, the student rights movement has created confusion and feelings of powerlessness among teachers. It is essential that teachers and school officials cut through the myths and rhetoric surrounding student discipline and develop a thorough knowledge of their own legal powers and responsibilities.

Notes to Chapter 5

1. *Ingraham v. Wright,* 430 U.S. 651 (1977).

2. *South Carolina Code,* Sec. 59-19-90(3).

3. *Illinois Revised Statutes Annotated,* Ch. 122, Sec. 10-22.6.

4. *Colorado Revised Statutes,* Sec. 22-33-106 (Cum. Supp., 1978).

5. *Connecticut General Statutes Annotated,* Sec. 10-233b (1979 Supp.).

6. *Georgia Code Annotated,* Sec.32-836 (1979 Supp.).

7. *Florida Statutes Annotated,* Sec. 871.01; *S.H.B. v. State,* 355 So. 2d 1176 (Supreme Ct. of Fla., 1977).

8. *Arkansas Statutes,* Sec. 80-1629.4 (1979 Supp.).

9. *Ill. Rev. Stat. Ann.,* Ch. 122, Sec. 24-24.

10. *Fla. Stat. Ann.,* Sec. 232.28.

11. *Epperson v. Arkansas,* 393 U.S. 97, 104 (1968).

12. *Miller v. School District,* 495 F. 2d 658, 667 (7th Cir., 1974).

13. *Wood v. Strickland,* 420 U.S. 308, 326 (1975).

14. *Tinker v. Des Moines School District,* 393 U.S. 503 (1969).

15. *Goss v. Lopez,* 419 U.S. 565 (1975).

16. *Linwood v. City of Peoria,* 463 F. 2d 743 (7th Cir., 1972); *People in the Interest of K.P.,* 514 P. 2d 1131 (Supreme Ct. of Colo., 1973); *Soglin v. Kauffman,* 418 F. 2d 163 (7th Cir., 1969).

17. *Gonzales v. McEuen,* 435 F. Supp. 460 (C.D. Calif., 1977); *Caldwell v. Cannaday,* 340 F. Supp. 835 (N.D. Texas, 1972).

18. *Hamer v. Board,* 383 N.E. 2d 231 (Ill. App., 1978).

19. *Fla. Stat. Ann.,* Sec. 230.23.

20. *Estaban v. Central Missouri State College,* 415 F. 2d 1077 (8th Cir., 1969); cert. denied, 398 U.S. 965 (1970). See also *Hasson v. Boothby, 318 F. Supp. 1183 (D. Mass., 1970)* and *Clements v. Board,* 585 P. 2d 197, 204 (Supreme Ct. of Wyo., 1978).

21. *Goss v. Lopez* at 581.

22. *Linwood v. City* at 769.

23. *Wexell v. Scott,* 276 N.E. 2d 735 (Ill. App., 1971); *Fertich v. Michener,* 11 N.E. 605 (Supreme Ct. of Ind., 1887).

24. *Wexell v. Scott* at 736.

25. *Fertich v. Michener* at 611.

26. *Fenton v. Stear,* 423 F. Supp. 767 (W.D. Pa. 1976).

27. *Fenton v. Stear* at 772.

28. *Ingraham v. Wright* at 678, 682.

29. See *Welch v. Board,* 358 N.E. 2d 1364 (Ill. App., 1977); *Fender v. School District,* 347 N.E. 2d 270 (Ill. App., 1976); *Kurtz v. Winston-Salem/Forsyth County Board of Education,* 250 S.E. 2d 718 (N.C. App., 1979). According to the *New York Times* ("Regents Decide Spanking Is Now School Option," February 29, 1980), New Jersey, Massachusetts, Maine, and Maryland ban corporal punishment. Statutes in New Jersey *(Statutes Annotated,* 18A: 6-1) and Massachusetts *(General Laws Annotated,* Ch. 71, Sec. 37G) specifically prohibit corporal punishment. A Maryland statute *(Education Code Annotated,* Sec. 7:305) forbids the state board of education to prohibit the use of corporal punishment in the public schools of 19 listed counties. Maryland's three largest counties (Baltimore, Montgomery, and Prince Georges) and the city of Baltimore are not included in the list. A Maine statute *(Revised Statutes Annotated,* Title 20, Sec. 918) protects teachers who use reasonable force to control or remove a student who creates a disturbance.

30. *Andreozzi v. Rubano,* 141 A. 2d 639 (Supreme Ct. of Errors of Conn., 1958) at 641.

31. *Ga. Code Ann.,* Sec. 32-836 (1979 Supp.).

32. *Simms v. School District,* 508 P. 2d 236 (Ore. App., 1973).

33. *Andreozzi v. Rubano; People v. DeLuro,* 308 N.E. 2d 196 (Ill. App., 1974). See also *Owens v. Kentucky,* 473 S.W. 2d 827 (Ky. App., 1971).

34. *Conn. Gen. Stat. Ann.,* Sec. 10-233b. See also *Maine Rev. Stat. Ann.,* Sec. 20-918; *N.J. Stat. Ann.,* Sec. 18A: 6-1.

35. *Minorics v. Phillipsburg Board of Education,* Decision of the N.J. Commissioner of Education (March 24, 1972), p. 86.

36. *California Education Code Annotated,* Sec. 48903.5 (1979 Supp.).

37. *Knight v. Board,* 348 N.E. 2d 299 (Ill. App., 1976).

38. *Hamer v. Board.*

39. *Hasson v. Boothby.*

40. *Zeller v. Donegal,* 517 F. 2d 600 (3rd Cir., 1975).

41. *Braesch v. DePasquale,* 265 N.W. 2d 842 (Supreme Ct. of Neb., 1978).

42. Ibid. at 581.

43. *Gonzales v. McEuen.* In *Morale v. Grigel,* 422 F. Supp. 988 (D. N.H., 1976), a district court's due-process requirements were significantly less demanding when it reviewed an expulsion.

44. *Md. Educ. Code Ann.,* Sec. 7-304 (Cum. Supp., 1979).

45. *New Hampshire Revised Statutes Annotated,* Sec. 193:13 (1977 Supp.).

46. *Wisconsin Statutes Annotated,* Sec. 120.13 (Cum. Supp. 1979).

47. *Coolidge v. New Hampshire,* 403 U.S. 443 (1971).

48. The California courts have held that school officials are private persons. Therefore, they are not governed by the rules applicable to searches by law-

enforcement officers. However, school authorities may not search a student without provocation. The purpose of a search must be within the scope of the duties of the school (maintain order, protect students), and the search must be reasonable in light of the circumstances. A student who is suspected of selling drugs can be forced to produce the bulging contents of his pockets. See *In Re Donaldson,* 75 Cal. Rptr. 220 (App., 1969); *In Re Fred C.,* 102 Cal. Rptr. 682 (App., 1972); *In Re Christopher W.,* 105 Cal. Rptr. 775 (App., 1973).

Courts in Georgia and New York have held that school officials are public officers but not law-enforcement officers. School authorities must have sufficient cause to justify a search, but they are not subject to the same restraints as police. See *State v. Young,* 216 S.E. 2d 586 (Supreme Ct. of Ga., 1975); *People v. Scott D.,* 358 N.Y.S. 2d 403 (Ct. of App., 1974); *People v. Singletary,* 372 N.Y.S. 2d 68 (Ct. of App., 1975).

A Maryland statute *(Educ. Code Ann.,* Sec. 7-30-307) authorizes a principal, assistant principal, or school security guard to "make a reasonable search of a student on the school premises if he has probable cause to believe that the student has in his possession an item, the possession of which is a criminal offense." Locker searches appear to require no justification.

The U.S. Supreme Court has held that evidence which police obtain illegally—with less than probable cause to justify a search—cannot be used in a criminal prosecution. This is called the "exclusionary rule." The New York Court of Appeals has held that "sufficient cause" justifies a search by school officials. Evidence that school authorities obtain with less than sufficient cause cannot be used in a criminal prosecution *(People v. Scott D.).* Courts in Illinois, Washington, and New Jersey have upheld the use of evidence in criminal prosecution which had been obtained with sufficient cause by school authorities. See *In Re Boykin,* 327 N.E. 2d 460 (Supreme Ct. of Ill., 1972); *State v. McKinnon,* 558 P. 2d 781 (Supreme Ct. of Wash., 1977); In Re G.C., 296 A. 2d 102 (N.J. Super., 1972).

Georgia and California courts have held that the exclusionary rule applies only to police searches; evidence obtained illegally by school officials may be used in criminal prosecutions. (See *State v. Young; In Re Donaldson.)* In contrast, Louisiana's Supreme Court has held that school officials must have probable cause to search and that the exclusionary rule is applicable. See *State v. Moro,* 307 So. 2d 317 (1975).

The standard for deciding the admissibility of evidence in school expulsion or suspension hearings is unclear. One federal court has held that a school may not use evidence against a student which was illegally obtained by police; see *Caldwell v. Cannaday.* A second federal court has ruled that the exclusionary rule applies only to criminal and not school proceedings; see *Morale v. Grigel.* A third federal court has held that evidence obtained by school officials acting with sufficient cause is admissible in an expulsion hearing; see *M. v. Ball-Chatham Board of Education,* 429 F. Supp. 288 (S.D. Ill., 1977).

49. *Picha v. Wielgos,* 410 F. Supp. 1214 (N.D. Ill., 1976). The precise role played by police in the school setting in any instance is subject to interpretation. The implications of the police presence for the applicable search standards and subsequent civil and criminal proceedings are not settled. In *State v. McKinnon* there was a very close relationship between the police and school authorities. Nevertheless, the court ruled that a questionable search and consequent arrest were legal. In *In Re Fred C.,* a California appeals court held that school officials could call on the services of police to conduct a search of a recalcitrant student. Because the police were acting as agents of a school official and not conducting a police investigation, the search was justified by a lesser standard than probable cause. The police search and arrest were legal. In *Doe v. Renfrow,* 475 F. Supp. 1012 (N.D. Ind., 1979) a U.S. district court held that the presence of police while school officials searched for drugs did not alter the basic function of the school officials' activities because there was prior agreement that police would not make arrests as a result of finding drugs on students. The implication is that the nature of the search would have been altered had there been no prior agreement.

In the near future, the unsettled status of the law will protect school officials from liability for all but the grossest violations of student search rights. Contrast *Doe v. Renfrow* with *M.M. v. Anker,* 477 F. Supp. 837 (E.D. N.Y., 1979).

50. *People v. Overton,* 301 N.Y.S. 2d 479 (Ct. of App., 1967); *In Re Donaldson.*

51. See *Rawlings v. Kentucky,* 100 S. Ct. 2556 (1980) _____ U.S. _____. Also *California v. Dalton,* 157 Cal. Rptr. 497 (Supreme Ct., 1979); cert. denied, 79-930.

52. In *Doe v. Renfrow,* a U.S. district court held that the use of drug-sniffing dogs was a minor intrusion and not a violation of students' constitutional rights. Recent drug-related incidents at the school had provided sufficient justification for school officials to order a class-by-class walk-through using drug-sniffing dogs. Students do not have a reasonable expectation of privacy when they are sitting in a classroom. The dogs were an aid to school administrators in the observation of students; thus, the presence of the dogs did not constitute search and did not require a warrant. Identification by the dogs gave school officials reasonable cause to request a student to empty her pockets but was not sufficient justification to order a body search. In *M.M. v. Anker,* 607 F. 2d 589 (2nd Cir., 1979), the U.S. Court of Appeals, Second Circuit (jurisdiction New York, Connecticut, and Vermont) held that it is reasonable for the courts to require school officials to show probable cause before they conduct a highly intensive invasion; for example, a strip search: "[As] the intrusiveness of the search intensifies, the standard of Fourth Amendment 'reasonableness' approaches probable cause, even in the school context."

53. *Picha v. Wielgos.*

54. A California appeals court held that a school official has no legal duty to issue a Miranda warning to a student (a warning that evidence obtained may be used against the student) before listening to a confession.

55. *Bellnier v. Lund,* 348 F. Supp. 47 (N.D. N.Y., 1977).

56. *R.R. v. Board,* 263 A. 2d 180 (N.J. Super., 1970).

57. *Clements v. Board.*

58. *Caldwell v. Cannaday* at 838. See also *M. v. Ball-Chatham* at 291.

59. See *Calif. Educ. Code Ann.,* Sec. 48900(e) (Cum. Supp., 1979); *Fla. Stat. Ann.,* Sec. 232.26(2).

60. *Fenton v. Stear.*

6.

ACADEMIC FREEDOM

Who determines what a teacher teaches? Who should? What role should the teacher play in determining what is taught? If everybody agreed on the answers to these questions, there would be no need to be concerned about academic freedom. In reality, of course, there are as many different answers to those questions as there are competing attempts to influence the curriculum.[1]

The teacher is at the vortex of many competing influences.[2] The teacher is the one who must pick and choose from among conflicting demands about what to teach and how to teach it, what to exclude and what to incorporate. And the teacher is the one who stands in front of the class and delivers.

Numerous factors influence what is taught. Among the most important are student interests, desires, and needs; local community interests, commitments, and prejudices; school board directives; departmental curricula; state curriculum mandates; and the teachers' own assessments of what belongs in the classroom. Less important, but still influential, are curriculum materials and textbooks, state and local groups and organizations, politicians, and the mass media.

The factors that influence the curriculum often tug in different directions. The local community and its representatives on the school board have the primary responsibility for defining the curriculum. Teachers are obliged to teach whatever the local community decides should be taught. Teachers also have a professional and legal obligation to incorporate state-mandated materials even if these are not explicitly included in the local curriculum. Because the larger society as represented by the state is often more diverse than the local district, it has an interest in broadening the local curriculum and preventing it from being too parochial or one-sided.

Students' interests and needs can contribute another dimension of conflict. Students must be prepared to live in a future community that is not likely to resemble their present environment. An education that simply passes on the values and prejudices of the past is incomplete. In some cases, students are so alienated from the present that teachers feel they must adopt unorthodox methods just to be able to communicate with their students.[3]

Occasionally, teachers' choices meet with disapproval. Parents object to something a teacher said. A local group finds this or that element of the curriculum offensive. The school administration reacts. The school board investigates.

The law and the courts recognize that the conflicting obligations of teachers make them vulnerable. Tenure laws are designed to ensure that teachers cannot be dismissed except for good cause and after fair due-process procedures. The First Amendment guarantees a teacher's right of free speech. The concept of academic freedom is the best protection for a teacher whose instructional decisions legitimately represent the larger interests of the state against narrow local interests or whose choices inadvertently offend the local community.

How the Courts View Academic Freedom

Judges have been eloquent in their defense of academic freedom. One of the most eloquent and consistent defenders of academic freedom, Supreme Court Justice Brennan, wrote:

> Our nation is deeply committed to safeguarding academic freedom, which is of transcendent value to all of us and not merely to the teachers concerned. That freedom is therefore a special concern of the First Amendment, which does not tolerate laws that cast a pall of orthodoxy over the classroom. . . . The classroom is peculiarly the "marketplace of ideas." The nation's future depends upon leaders trained through wide exposure to that robust exchange of ideas which discovers truth "out of a multitude of tongues, [rather] than through any kind of authoritative selection."[4]

The opinion that the school must expose students to a wide

range of perspectives is reflected in lower-court decisions as well. In addition, in *Mailloux v. Kiley,* U.S. District Court Chief Judge Charles Wyzanski noted that in a free society the teacher serves as a model of the rational decision-making citizen:

> Our national belief is that the heterodox as well as the orthodox are a source of individual and of social growth. We do not confine academic freedom to conventional teachers or to those who can get a majority vote from their colleagues. Our faith is that the teacher's freedom to choose among options for which there is any substantial support will increase his intellectual vitality and his moral strength. The teacher whose responsibility has been nourished by independence, enterprise, and free choice becomes for his student a better model of the democratic citizen. His examples of applying and adapting the values of the old order to the demands and opportunities of a constantly changing world are among the most important lessons he gives to youth.[5]

The teacher may be a model of intellectual enterprise and reasoned choice, but school boards have the authority to determine classroom standards. However, as Judge Irving R. Kaufman of the U.S. Court of Appeals, Second Circuit, wrote, school officials must exercise restraint:

> The dangers of unrestrained discretion are readily apparent. Under the guise of beneficent concern for the welfare of school children, school authorities, albeit unwittingly, might permit prejudices of the community to prevail. It is in such a situation that the will of the transient majority can prove devastating to freedom of expression.[6]

The curriculum is not limited to what is in the lesson book. Some judges have recognized that it may be useful or even necessary for a teacher to go beyond the formal curriculum. As Judge Thomas Fairchild of the Court of Appeals, Seventh Circuit, wrote, albeit in dissent:

> A teacher may be more successful with his students if he is able to relate to them in philosophy of life, and, conversely, students may profit by learning something of a teacher's views on general subjects. Academic freedom entails the exchange of ideas which promote education in its broadest sense.[7]

Not all the rhetoric and reason are on one side. Judges have also argued persuasively that there are limits to academic freedom. In a concurring opinion to the Supreme Court's Epperson "monkey trial" case, Justice Hugo Black wrote:

> I am also not ready to hold that a person hired to teach school children takes with him into the classroom a constitutional right to teach sociological, economic, political, or religious subjects that the school's managers do not want discussed. This court has said that the rights of free speech, "while fundamental in our democratic society, still do not mean that everyone with opinions or beliefs to express may address a group at any public place and at any time." I question whether it is absolutely certain, as the court's opinion indicates, that "academic freedom" permits a teacher to breach his contractual agreement to teach only the subjects designated by the school authorities who hired him.[8]

And in an angry dissent to the Tinker armband decision, Black articulated a perspective that many share:

> In my view, teachers in state-controlled public schools are hired to teach there. . . . Certainly a teacher is not paid to go into school and teach subjects the state does not hire him to teach as a part of its selected curriculum.[9]

A somewhat softer view was expressed by Judge Frank N. Johnson, when he sat as Chief Judge on the U.S. District Court in Alabama:

> The right of academic freedom, however, like all other constitutional rights, is not absolute and must be balanced against the competing interests of society. This court is keenly aware of the state's vital interest in protecting the impressionable minds of its young people from *any* form of extreme propagandism in the classroom.[10]

Keefe v. Geanakos[11]

Robert Keefe, a creative high school English teacher, believed he should expose students to relevant contemporary writing.

In September 1969, he distributed copies of a recent issue of Atlantic *magazine, which contained an article by Robert Jay Lifton entitled "The Young and the Old: Notes on a New History." The article was an analysis of the different perspectives that the young and old bring to history. One part of the article examined the origin of the rallying cry of the Columbia University rebellion, "Up against the wall, M----- F-----!" Keefe told his students that if any were offended by the vocabulary they could do an alternate assignment.*

Some parents protested the use of a profanity in the lesson, and members of the school board asked Keefe if he would agree not to use the word again in his class. He replied that he could not, in good conscience, agree to their request, and he was suspended.

After hearing the case, the court concluded that (1) in the context of the article, the word was not obscene nor libidinous; (2) use of the word in the discussion of the article was necessary to explore the thesis of the article; (3) high school seniors are old enough to be exposed to such language; and (4) no school regulation existed which would have notified the teacher that the word was forbidden; indeed, school library books contained similar words.

Webb v. Lake Mills Community School District [12]

Martha Webb was discharged as a high school drama coach for allowing vulgarity in play rehearsals and for choosing plays that contained vulgarity and drinking scenes. When she began serving as drama coach, Webb knew that school officials had been unhappy the year before when the former coach had produced Brigadoon and I Remember Mama. These productions were criticized for their irreverence, vulgarity, and drinking scenes. However, the coach was not fired, but resigned for unrelated reasons.

School officials believed that when they hired Webb they had told her that absolutely no drinking nor swearing was to be portrayed in plays. Webb recalled being told that plays should not contain unnecessary or excessive drinking or vulgarity of the sort that had characterized the previous year's plays. School board regulations had no specific policy prohibiting profanity and drinking scenes in plays, nor was there a policy precluding the use of materials that contained profanity, vulgarity, or drinking.

The court found that the superintendent had not voiced objections when he overheard swearing during rehearsals, nor had parents or spectators complained when the plays were presented. The only disruption was precipitated by school officials.

The court concluded that, while profanity was not essential to proper teaching, Webb was in good faith in believing that the use of such words had the legitimate purpose of imparting knowledge of drama. The substitution of "darn" and "son of a biscuit" for less-acceptable terms in the actual production was consistent with her agreement not to use excessive vulgarity.

The court said: "A public high school teacher has a sub-

stantive right to choose a teaching method which serves a
demonstrated educational purpose and a procedural right not
to be discharged for use of a teaching method which is not
proscribed by a regulation."

Unfortunately, many teachers have found themselves in trouble for using "dirty words." Such cases are interesting from two perspectives. First, they reflect a form of hypocrisy: words which are used by students at home, in the street, and in the school halls are taboo for the teacher. Even efforts by teachers to develop meaningful lessons around the use of profanity and vulgarity and to force corrective consciousness on students have engendered controversy.[13] Second, only words—not ideas—are attacked, in contrast to other cases that involve unpopular ideas which challenge the community and its prejudices.

Epperson v. Arkansas[14]

A 1925 Arkansas law forbade public school teachers "to teach the theory or doctrine that mankind is ascended or descended from a lower order of animals." The Little Rock schools adopted a new biology text which included a chapter on evolution. Susan Epperson, the tenth-grade biology teacher at Central High, had to decide whether to teach the statutorily condemned chapter. She decided to teach the theory of evolution, and she sought a court injunction to prevent enforcement of the law.

The Chancery Court, where she began proceedings, held that the law violated the First and Fourteenth amendments. However, on appeal, the Arkansas Supreme Court ruled that the statute was constitutional. On further appeal to the U.S. Supreme Court, the majority found that the law violated the establishment of religion clause because the motivation for the law was the advancement of a particular religious creed.

The court went on to say: "The state's undoubted right to prescribe the curriculum for its public schools does not carry with it the right to prohibit, on pain of criminal penalty, the teaching of a scientific theory or doctrine where that prohibition is based upon reasons that violate the First Amendment. It is much too late to argue that the State may impose upon the teachers in its schools any conditions that it chooses, however restrictive they may be of constitutional guarantees."

Sterzing v. School District[15]

Henry Keith Sterzing taught senior political science and civics at John Foster Dulles High School in Stafford, Texas.

In September, the principal told Sterzing that he had received some parental complaints. Specifically, he had been told that in response to a student's question, Sterzing had said that he did not personally oppose interracial marriage.

In subsequent conversations, Sterzing's department head and members of the school board encouraged him to confine his teaching to the text and to avoid controversial issues. He responded that it was impossible to teach a senior class in current events and avoid controversy. School authorities gave him no definite instructions.

In February Sterzing taught a short unit on race relations, using materials cleared through and ordered by the school. Parents complained to the school board that the materials were propagandistic and biased. Sterzing was discharged immediately without a hearing.

The U.S. District Court concluded that the school board had denied Sterzing procedural and substantive due process. Furthermore, through its arbitrary actions, the board had denied him his right to free speech. School officials presented no evidence to suggest that Sterzing's classroom methods strayed from professionally accepted standards.

The judge wrote: "A teacher's methods are not without limits. . . . On the other hand, a teacher must not be manacled with rigid regulations, which preclude full adaptation of the course to the times in which we live. It would be ill advised to presume that a teacher would be limited, in essence, to a single textbook. . . . The court finds Mr. Sterzing's objectives in his teaching to be proper to stimulate critical thinking, to create an awareness of our present political and social community, and to enliven the educational process. These are desirable goals."

Wilson v. Chancellor[16]

Since 1971, Dean Wilson, a political science instructor at Molalla Union High School in Oregon, had been inviting speakers representing a cross-section of political viewpoints to address his students. In May 1975, in response to community pressure, the school board cancelled Wilson's invitation to a self-professed Communist.

The board had first tried to minimize public objections by creating special conditions for the Communist speaker. They required that students be shown the anti-Communist film Nightmare in Red, *that anti-Communist speakers be scheduled before and after the Communist presentation, and that students not wishing to hear the Communist be excused. After additional protests, the board gave up and simply*

> *banned all political speakers from appearing at the high school.*
>
> *Wilson sued in the U.S. District Court under the civil rights act to obtain judicial relief from infringement of his rights of free speech, academic freedom, and equal protection of the law.*
>
> *The court ruled that teaching method is a form of expression protected by the First Amendment. Considered in the light of the special circumstances of the school, the restraints were unreasonable. The school board could not justify a ban on political speakers as inappropriate to high school students, especially since Oregon law mandated teaching government. Furthermore, the ban discriminated against political speakers and the teaching of politically oriented subjects by prohibiting only political speakers. Finally, in fact, the board had allowed all speakers except the Communist.*
>
> *The judge concluded: "A course designed to teach students that a free and democratic society is superior to those in which freedoms are sharply curtailed will fail entirely if it fails to teach one important lesson: that the power of the state is never so great that it can silence a man or woman simply because there are those who disagree."*

Academic freedom, as noted earlier, is the judicial refuge of teachers when, in legitimately representing the broad interests of education, their instructional choices inadvertently offend the local community. We can examine the cases described from this perspective.

In the Epperson, Wilson and Sterzing cases, society at large had an interest in imposing a broader view on the community. Epperson set out to test the law against teaching alternatives to the theory of divine creation. Wilson sued to force the local school board to permit him to teach in accordance with state mandates and the constitutional rights of citizens. The Sterzing case parallels Wilson's. Sterzing was called on the carpet for teaching current events to children whose parents did not want them to know what was happening.

In all the cases but Epperson's, the teachers did not deliberately set out to provoke school officials or their communities. Keefe, Webb, and Wilson might well have altered their intentions had they anticipated controversy. Keefe felt that he could not back away from using the article after he had introduced it to the students. Webb thought that her choices were consistent with the instructions of her supervisors. Wilson had been inviting speakers to class for several years without objections from the community. Even Sterzing thought that his supervisors respected his position; they did not explicitly order him to alter his teaching program.

Academic freedom came to the aid of these teachers. Teachers have the right to make significant decisions about what and how they teach. Nevertheless, there are limits to this right, and it is linked with three basic responsibilities:

• A teacher should not act so as to disrupt the school or incite students to do so.[17] There is *no excuse* for disruption, and courts will not abide it. In each case, described here, the court was aware that the educational process had not been disrupted as a result of the teacher's challenge to school officials.

• A teacher should not go beyond clearly stated limits to instructional discretion or violate explicit rules. Teachers cannot substitute their own judgments for the opinions of supervisors or state curriculum mandates. Only Epperson challenged a clear rule, and she did so by going to court to seek an injunction.

• A teacher should not use profanity. Profanity in the classroom is bound to cause a stir. Such words are calculated to shock; however, context affects the shock value of words. Profanity heard in a street or bar generally has less shock value than the same word when heard in a classroom. And a phrase used during a discussion in the classroom may have less shock value than the same phrase when it is repeated at home or on the phone to a school board member. In each case cited here, the court examined the context in which the controversial material was used.

Disruption, insubordination, and profanity are limiting factors in any consideration of academic freedom. Nevertheless, in hearing cases involving academic freedom, courts will take into account specific surrounding circumstances and attempt to gauge the seriousness of the teachers' actions. Courts will also generally consider the maturity of the students, professional opinion, and the relevance of the controversial item to the course.

Maturity of students. There is a consensus that a senior high school teacher has more discretion in exposing students to controversial ideas. After all, 18-year-olds are legally adults in many states. Courts presume that older students are more sophisticated than younger students. They are better equipped to identify propaganda and better able to examine new ideas, within the context of what they have already learned. Finally, the courts presume that older students have had sufficient exposure to hard-core profanity that they will be neither shocked nor damaged by hearing or reading it in class.

Keefe, Sterzing, and Wilson taught upper-division courses. Webb's students represented a cross-section of grade levels, but she made special efforts to shield them from excessive profanity. It was the Little Rock school board, not Epperson, who decided that tenth-graders were mature enough to be exposed to biology.

Weight of professional opinion. Academic freedom is a claim based on the professional judgment of the teacher. Thus, the court looks to the profession to justify the claim. A teacher benefits from the support of professional authorities. Even professionals in the same field often disagree, however. Although it would certainly help any teacher to have the unanimous support of the profession, courts do not expect unanimity. Each of the teachers whose cases are described here was following accepted professional practices.

Relevance of the controversial item to the course. Every course has content and goals which are more or less specified in advance. Courts do not expect teachers to be individual entrepreneurs. Teachers are expected to stay within the curriculum outline. Therefore, if a teacher is to be protected by academic freedom, there must be some legitimate link between the controversial material and the basic curriculum. Such links are evident in each of the cases discussed. For Keefe and Webb, the profanity was intrinsic to a legitimate intellectual endeavor. Although the teachers might have chosen other works, the readings they chose were clearly related to the basic curricula and to the goals of their courses. Similarly, Epperson, Sterzing, and Wilson dealt with issues that clearly were germane to their courses.

These are the major considerations that guide the courts in attempting to balance the rights of teachers, the needs of students, and the interests of school officials. Few teachers who meet these criteria face serious problems. They can expect to be supported by the courts. Even teachers who fail to meet one or more of these standards may prevail in the courts. Cases involving the use of profanity are apt examples. Judges start out with the belief that profanity does not belong in the schools. Nevertheless, they are willing to consider its educational relevance and contextual usage.

In contrast, disruption is a cardinal sin. The courts have no sympathy for teachers who incite their students to insubordination or who disrupt ordinary school processes. Similarly, the courts have seldom backed a teacher who rejected clear instructions from supervisors concerning the curriculum or materials. Teachers should seek the aid of the courts and not act in outright defiance of supervisors.

The limits that the courts have placed on academic freedom are clear in cases where the courts refused to back the teacher.

Ahern v. Grand Island School District [18]

Frances Ahern, a 12th-grade economics teacher, was experimenting with a new teaching method. She allowed students to make decisions customarily made by teachers. These decisions included subjects for daily discussion, course material, and rules of classroom behavior. While Ahern was away on leave for a week, her substitute attempted to impose unaccustomed discipline on the class, and slapped a student in the process.

When Ahern returned on Monday, she reacted angrily. She said, "That b----, I hope if this happens again all of you will walk out." Further, she attempted to repair the damage by discussing the incident with her students and working with them to formulate a new corporal punishment regulation.

On Wednesday, Ahern's principal reprimanded her for her intemperate language and told her to stop discussing the incident, get back to teaching economics, and use more-conventional teaching methods. Despite these explicit instructions, Ahern continued to talk about the issue with her classes and asked the principal to come to class to discuss the proposed new regulations. On Friday, students engaged in a nondisruptive preschool demonstration.

Ahern was fired. She went to court and claimed denial of her right to speak, her right to teach, and due process. The U.S. Court of Appeals ruled that Miss Ahern was invested by the Constitution with no right either (1) to persist in a course of teaching behavior which contravened the valid dictates of her employers . . . regarding classroom method or (2) to teach politics in a course in economics.

The Ahern case contains the ingredients of many of the academic freedom cases which teachers have lost. Ahern lost because she persisted in a course of teaching despite explicit instructions to desist. Discussions of corporal punishment were unrelated to the normal class subject. Her behavior was disruptive, and she encouraged disruptive behavior among her students.

Nigosian v. Weiss[19]

The Gibraltar School District was involved in an acrimonious labor dispute between the teachers and the school board. In an effort to isolate the school children from possible detrimental effects, school officials ordered that there be no classroom discussion of the dispute without permission of the school principal.

Richard Nigosian, a fifth-grade teacher, was fired because he allowed his class to discuss the dispute. In upholding his dismissal, the U.S. District Court said that a school board has the right to set the curriculum and the responsibility to protect students from disruptive influences. Teachers should refrain from discussing subjects not germane to the program of instruction. The board did not infringe on Nigosian's rights but merely required him to obtain proper authorization before speaking to his students about a subject of little educational value. Nigosian had other means available to express his views.

Harris v. Mechanicville Central School District[20]

For several years, William Harris had taught J.D. Salinger's Catcher in the Rye *to his sophomore English class without incident. However, one fall, parental complaints led the superintendent of schools to question Harris's methods, particularly the use of explicit street language in the classroom. Harris and the superintendent discussed this complaint, and Harris voluntarily agreed to drop the book.*

The next fall, without warning and despite the earlier agreement, Harris used the book again. He was summoned to the principal's office. After five minutes, Harris abruptly walked out despite the principal's request that he return. Harris was fired for two counts of insubordination.

The New York Court of Appeals ruled that the issue was not academic freedom. This was not an instance of a teacher's defending the use of a book and firmly standing his ground against community pressure. Instead, there was substantial evidence that he had agreed to stop teaching the novel and subsequently violated that agreement. Further, without an acceptable excuse, he had walked out on the conference with the principal.

While Harris's misdeeds were not trivial, his punishment was disproportionate to his offenses. He had not been morally delinquent, nor were his actions consistent with a pattern of unwillingness to accept direction. A one-year suspension without pay would have been more than ample punishment, the court said.

Palmer v. Board of Education of Chicago[21]

The kindergarten curriculum of the Chicago public schools calls for children to learn the Pledge of Allegiance and other patriotic rituals and songs. Children are also supposed to learn about holidays as they occur through the school year.

When Joethelia Palmer was hired to teach kindergarten, she told her principal that her religious convictions as a Jehovah's Witness would not permit her to teach anything having to do with love of country, the flag, or patriotism. The principal attempted to accommodate Palmer's convictions, and arranged for other teachers and parents to instruct her students in patriotism.

However, Palmer refused to lead activities related to Columbus Day, Halloween, Thanksgiving, Christmas, and the birthdays of prominent Americans. She considered it idolatry to teach about Abraham Lincoln and why Americans observe his birthday. Consequently, her students entered first grade inadequately prepared, and parents were upset. Some parents threatened to withhold their children from her class.

At the beginning of the new school year, the principal told Palmer that she would have to teach the children the words to the Pledge of Allegiance as well as those of "America" and other patriotic songs. Further, she would have to teach and conduct activities surrounding commonly observed holidays in order that "children learn the ethos of all people and develop tolerance and appreciation."

Palmer said that she would not comply. When she was dismissed, Palmer sued the school system for violating her right to freedom of religion.

The court observed that freedom of religion is fundamental; only a compelling state interest may infringe on religious freedom. Clearly, Palmer had the right to her beliefs. She may have had the right to refuse to say the Pledge of Allegiance. However, she was not free to disregard the prescribed curriculum. The state, acting through local school boards, has the power to teach students the values of the community. When balanced against disruption of the school and the legitimate goal of inculcating the children with patriotic values, Palmer's religious freedom was secondary.

The courts upheld her dismissal.

Wasilewski v. Board[22]

Edwin M. Wasilewski, a highly regarded tenured teacher at Milwaukee's Boy's Tech High School, taught two 12th-grade speech classes. In his classes, he discussed houses of *prostitution. He walked from desk to desk and told each boy whether he looked old enough to gain admittance. He told vulgar stories. He described the act of breaking the hymen of a virgin and implied that he was speaking from personal experience. Finally, he discussed premarital sex without indicating that it was against state laws.*

Wisconsin law says that teachers may be dismissed for conduct which transgresses the bounds of good behavior or which constitutes inefficiency. Wasilewski was dismissed. He appealed to the courts, contending that he had violated no specific rules or warnings.

In reviewing administrative actions, the court said, the rule is that "findings of the board upon the facts before it are conclusive if in any reasonable view the evidence sustains them." Here the findings of fact amply supported the charge of lack of good behavior. Wasilewski had gone beyond the bounds of propriety.

Limits on the Powers of School Officials

First Amendment freedoms are fragile. They need breathing space to survive. Thus, the courts permit some latitude to those who exercise freedom of speech.[23] Academic freedom gives teachers some discretion in judging whether material is suitable for or relevant to instruction. Given the presumption of some latitude, the courts have said that teachers cannot be punished for conduct involving First Amendment rights unless the conduct has been proscribed in clear and precise terms.

Need for Prior Notice

One of the strongest defenses that a teacher can mount in an academic freedom case is lack of notice. The courts recognize that teachers are professionals who act in a sensitive area. They appreciate the need to give teachers discretion in making instructional choices and shield them from the fear that higher authorities will issue an after-the-fact ruling against them. The California Supreme Court remarked in *Morrison v. California:*

Teachers, particularly in the light of their professional expertise, will normally be able to determine what kind of conduct indicates unfitness to teach. Teachers are further protected by the fact that they cannot be disciplined merely because they made a reasonable, good faith, professional judgment in the course of their employment with which higher authorities later disagreed.[24]

The absence of prior notice was a factor that worked in the favor of Keefe, Sterzing, and Webb. In the Webb case, the court found that school officials had failed to give clear and precise directions to the new drama coach. In the Sterzing decision, the court was careful to note that his supervisors, though concerned about his teaching of controversial issues, had not given him definite instructions. In contrast, Ahern was given specific instructions to stop discussing corporal punishment and get on with her economics lessons. She was punished, not for her intemperate outburst, but for her persistent defiance and disruption. Similarly, in unilaterally deciding to resume the use of *Catcher in the Rye,* Harris defied legitimate school authority. His defiance, however, was a solitary and nondisruptive act.

Warning or notice is not always necessary. The court held that Wasilewski had gone far beyond the boundaries of good taste and judgment. His professional training and good sense should have restrained his actions. Prior notice was not required.

First Amendment Freedoms

The state and the local community are endowed with the responsibility for setting the school curriculum. This is established law. School boards and school administrators have the authority to define the curriculum. Thus, the focus of this discussion has been on the function of academic freedom as a defensive shield to protect teachers who inadvertently provoke criticism and whose professional judgments are challenged. It would be a mistake to conclude, however, that the First Amendment can be abrogated by prior notice or explicit prohibitions from supervisors.

Academic freedom acts as a restraint on the powers of the community and its representatives on the school board. As noted in our discussion of the Epperson case, the Supreme Court majority held that the state may not violate First Amendment rights in prescribing the curriculum. Justice Abe Fortas wrote, "It is much too late to argue the state may impose . . . any conditions . . . however restrictive they may be of constitutional guarantees."[25] In his concurring opinion, Justice Potter Stewart identified what he thought was one limit on the state. "A state is entirely free, for example, to decide that the only foreign language in its public school system shall be Spanish. But would a state be constitutionally free to punish a teacher for letting his students know that other languages are also spoken in the world? I think not.''

What are the limits on the discretion of school authorities? The Epperson, Wilson, Sterzing, and Keefe decisions illustrate some of the limits. School officials may use a variety of decisional bases for selecting subjects to include in the curriculum, but the Epperson ruling said that some kinds of reasons are unacceptable. Specifically, religious doctrine cannot dictate the curriculum. In the Wilson case, the court said that local community prejudices could not subvert the intentions or interests of the state. The Sterzing ruling said that when school officials employ a teacher to teach a course they should not (though it is not clear that they could not) limit his freedom to use appropriate professional tools and skills.[27] In Keefe, the court ruled that although school officials or parents may be unhappy about the use of a specific word or article, a teacher has a right to use relevant material under appropriate circumstances.[28]

Rational Basis for Restrictions

Some recent cases dealing with library censorship suggest that the courts are gradually establishing an additional limit on the discretion of school officials. Several courts have maintained that the criteria for selecting or rejecting material must be rational or the result of a systematic procedure. There are many reasons why school authorities may choose one book or topic over another.[29] Libraries have physical limits; the school day is short; there is much to teach and learn. The community may prefer to emphasize particular topics or values. As long as the decision is not clearly unreasonable, the courts will not substitute its judgment for that of school officials.

Some criteria, however—particularly those that implicate First Amendment values—may require more than a rational basis.[30] A Massachusetts district court has ruled that local school officials must demonstrate substantial or legitimate government interest in order to justify censorship.[31] The Tinker case established that schools cannot suppress student expression unless the forbidden conduct threatens to interfere substantially with the school's function. It follows, the Massachusetts court held, that school officials must demonstrate some need on the order of school discipline in order to justify censorship.

The Sixth Circuit Court of Appeals issued a similar ruling in an Ohio case. The Strongsville Board of Education voted to remove *Cat's Cradle* and *Catch 22* from the school library. The court concluded that the books were removed because the board found their content objectionable and distasteful. The court ruled that the board could not "place conditions on the use of the library which were related solely to the social or political tastes of school board members."[32]

The difference between personal taste and reasoned judgment may not always be clear. As noted, courts recognize the authority of school officials to determine the basic curriculum. Distinguishing the good from the bad, the sound from the unsound, the classics from the trash *is not censorship.* Nevertheless, even those courts that have accepted, in the guise of "selecting and winnowing," what looks to many like censorship have been at pains to emphasize that nothing like the thought-control measures challenged in Epperson are involved.[33] Teachers remain free to discuss books. Students remain free to buy and read books. No system of thought is outlawed or unmentionable.

In summary, teachers are expected to use good judgment. They may not disrupt the educational process; they should not substitute their own judgments for those of their supervisors; and they generally should not use profanity or vulgar language. When a teacher's judgment is challenged, the courts will consider the maturity of the students, the weight of professional opinion, and the relevance of the challenged materials or activity to the course.

The absence of prior notice can give a teacher the benefit of the doubt. Additionally, evidence that supervisors knew of, acceded to, or supported the controversial curriculum choice should absolve the teacher of responsibility. Teachers who intend to use material or techniques which they think might be controversial should first obtain the support of their supervisors. Even a minimal level of supervisory awareness and approval of the teacher's activities can shield a teacher from harmful attacks.

Prior notice or prohibition by supervisors does not eliminate academic freedom. State and school officials are limited as to the kinds of conditions they impose on the constitutional rights of teachers and students. The courts are available to teachers and students whose rights are violated.

Teachers require latitude and discretion. Freedom of expression and the educational needs of students demand a certain amount of instructional discretion. As a recent Court of Appeals decision noted, teachers cannot be made to read from a script prepared or approved by the school board: "Censorship or suppression of expression of opinion even in the classroom should be tolerated only when there is a legitimate interest in the state which can be said to require priority."[34]

Notes to Chapter 6

1. For some major articles on the academic freedom of primary and secondary teachers, see Goldstein, "The Asserted Constitutional Right of Public School Teachers to Determine What They Teach," *University of Pennsylvania Law Review* 124 (1976), p. 1293; and Nahmod, "Controversy in the Classroom: The High School Teacher and Freedom of Expression," *George Washington Law Review* 39 (1971), p. 1032.

2. Joel F. Henning et al., *Mandate for Change: The Impact of Law on Educational Innovation* (Chicago: American Bar Association, Social Science Education Consortium, and ERIC Clearinghouse on Educational Management, 1979).

3. *East Hartford Education Association v. School District,* 562 F. 2d 838 (2nd Cir., 1977).

4. *Keyishian v. Board of Regents,* 385 U.S. 589, 603 (1967). See also *Wieman v. Updegraff,* 344 U.S. 183, 195-196 (1952).

5. *Mailloux v. Kiley,* 323 F. Supp. 1387, 1391 (D. Mass, 1971); affirmed, 448 F. 2d 1242 (1st. Cir., 1971).

6. *James v. Board,* 461 F. 2d 566, 575 (2nd Cir., 1972).

7. *Brubaker v. Board,* 502 F 2d 973, 991 (7th Cir., 1974).

8. *Epperson v. Arkansas,* 393 U.S. 97, 113, 114 (1968).

9. *Tinker v. Des Moines School District,* 393 U.S. 503, 521, 522 (1968).

10. *Parducci v. Rutland,* 316 F. Supp. 352, 355 (M.D. Ala., 1970).

11. *Keefe v. Geanakos,* 418 F. 2d 359 (1st Cir., 1969). For cases with similar circumstances, see *Lindros v. Governing Board,* 108 Cal. Rptr. 185 (Supreme Ct., 1973); *Board of Trustees v. Metzger,* 104 Cal. Rptr. 452 (Supreme Ct., 1972).

12. *Webb v. Lake Mills Community School District,* 344 F. Supp. 791 (N.D. Iowa, 1972).

13. See *Central York School District v. Erhart,* 387 A. 2d 1006 (Pa. Cmwlth., 1978) and *Mailloux v. Kiley.*

14. *Epperson v. Arkansas.*

15. *Sterzing v. Ft. Bend Independent School District,* 376 F. Supp. 657 (S.D. Tex., 1972); remanded for determination of proper remedy, 496 F. 2d 92 (5th Cir., 1974).

16. *Wilson v. Chancellor,* 418 F. Supp. 1358 (D. Ore., 1976). For contrast, see *Mercer v. Michigan State Board of Education,* 379 F. Supp. 582 (W.D. Mich.).

17. For examples of the courts' perspective on teacher disruption, see *Birdwell v. Hazelwood School District,* 352 F. Supp. 613 (E.D. Mo., 1972); *Petitions of John Davenport et al.,* 283 A. 2d 452 (Supreme Ct. of Vt., 1971); *Gilbertson v. McAlister,* 403 F. Supp. 1 (D. Conn., 1975).

18. *Ahern v. Grand Island School District,* 456 F. 2d 399 (8th Cir., 1972). Also see *Goldwasser v. Brown,* 417 F. 2d 1169 (D.C. Cir., 1969).

19. *Nigosian v. Weiss,* 343 F. Supp. 757 (E.D. Mich., 1971). Also see *Clark v. Holmes,* 474 F. 2d 928 (7th Cir., 1972); cert. denied, 411 U.S. 972 (1973).

20. *Harris v. Mechanicville Central School District,* 382 N.Y.S. 2d 251 (Supreme Ct., 1976); reversed, 394 N.Y.S. 2d 302 (A.D., 1977); affirmed as modified, 408 N.Y.S. 2d 384 (Ct. of Appeals, 1978).

21. *Palmer v. Board of Education of Chicago,* 466 F. Supp. 600 (N.D. Ill., 1979); affirmed, 603 F. 2d 1271 (7th Cir., 1979); cert. denied, 100 S. Ct. 689(4) (1980).

22. *Wasilewski v. Board,* 111 N.W. 2d 198 (Supreme Ct. of Wis., 1961); appeal dismissed, 360 U.S. 720 (1962). See also *De Caprio v. Redmond,* 350 N.E. 2d 119 (Ill. App., 1976). Compare with *Mailloux v. Kiley* and *Brubaker v. Board.* See also *Root v. Board,* 399 N.Y.S. 2d 785 (A.D., 1977).

23. *NAACP v. Button,* 371 U.S. 415, 433 (1963).

24. *Morrison v. State Board of Education,* 82 Cal. Rptr. 175 (Supreme Ct., 1969).

25. *Epperson v. Arkansas* at 107.

26. Ibid. at 116.

27. See also *Cary v. Board,* 598 F. 2d 535, 543 (10th Cir., 1979).

28. *Keefe v. Geanakos* at 361-362: "Hence the question in this case is whether a teacher may, for demonstrated educational purposes, quote a 'dirty' word. . . . With the greatest of respect to such parents, their sensibilities are not the full measure of what is proper education."

29. *Presidents Council District 25 v. Community School Board No. 25,* 457 F. 2d 289, 291 (2d Cir., 1972); cert. denied, 409 U.S. 998.

30. See *Presidents Council v. Community* at 293:

   The administration of any library, whether it be a university or particularly a public junior high school, involves a constant process of selection and winnowing based not only on educational needs but financial and architectural realities. To suggest that the shelving or unshelving of books presents a constitutional issue, *particularly where there is no showing of a curtailment of freedom of speech or thought,* is a proposition we cannot accept. [Emphasis added.]

31. *Right to Read Defense Committee of Chelsea v. School Committee of the City of Chelsea,* 454 F. Supp. 703, 712, 713 (D. Mass., 1978). See also *Cary v. Board* at 543.

32. *Minarcini v. Strongsville City School District,* 541 F. 2d 577, 582 (6th Cir., 1976). The court conceded that the decision was reasoned (at 580) but rejected the reasons as violating the First Amendment rights of students to receive information.

33. See especially *Bicknell v. Vergennes Union High School,* 475 F. Supp. 615, 621 (D. Ver., 1979). Also see *Cary v. Board* at 543 and *Minarcini v. Strongsville* at 582.

34. *Cary v. Board* at 543.

7.
FREEDOM
OF SPEECH
AND ASSOCIATION

Can a public school teacher criticize the school board? Make a speech in favor of higher pay? Advocate war, peace, or Christian love? Organize a union, a teach-in, or a sit-in? How does tenure affect First Amendment rights?

The First Amendment to the U.S. Constitution says, in part, "Congress shall make no law abridging freedom of speech or the right of the people peaceably to assemble and petition the government." Under the *due-process clause* of the Fourteenth Amendment, the First Amendment applies to states and their subdivisions, including school districts.

These freedoms are precious to all Americans and especially so to teachers. As intelligent, educated, involved members of the community, teachers are likely to make use of the opportunities these freedoms protect. As people responsible for instructing impressionable youth in a highly visible setting, teachers are likely to be scrutinized in terms of their personal behavior. As public employees, teachers have sometimes been vulnerable to intimidation.

First Amendment freedoms may be more important to teachers now and in the near future than they were a relatively short time ago.

The accelerating and expanding efforts of teacher organizations give more teachers a stake in freedom of association. The pressures of RIF, retrenchment, and inflation have encouraged many teachers to take a more-active interest in school board decisions. International pressures, as represented by Iranian hostilities and Russian expansionism, may increase demands for political conformity.

Freedom of Association

The right to associate may be the teacher's most important right. Few teachers are orators, and few individual teachers feel a need to speak out or petition. However, it is often useful or necessary for individuals to band together in an attempt to influence policies. On such occasions, it is important to have not only the right to associate with a group but also the right to disassociate one's self from particular positions or activities of the group.

Teachers have a right to associate with and join groups, including teachers' associations and unions. Further, individual members cannot be held responsible for positions or acts of a group of which they are unaware or in which they did not participate. The U.S. Supreme Court has confirmed these rights in three landmark decisions going back to the 1950s.

In *Wieman v. Updegraff* (1953), the court said that a state could not classify innocent association with knowing association. The decision was a response to a challenge to an Oklahoma loyalty oath statute that made membership in a so-called subversive organization grounds for dismissal from public employment. The court said that the law was unconstitutional: public employees could not be fired "solely on the basis of organizational membership, regardless of their knowledge concerning the organizations. . . ."[1]

The Supreme Court went further in protecting the freedom to associate in *Shelton v. Tucker* (1960). Shelton challenged an Arkansas law that required teachers to file annual affidavits listing organizational memberships and contributions. This was clearly an attempt to intimidate the teachers, to discourage teachers from joining or contributing to any group. The court said: "The vigilant protection of constitutional freedoms is nowhere more vital than in the community of American schools."[2] The Arkansas statute went beyond legitimate inquiry into the fitness and competence of teachers.

Keyishian v. New York Board of Regents (1967) is the capstone in the evolution of the right of association. Here, a teacher challenged a Board of Regents rule that made membership in an organization on a subversive list *prima facie* evidence for disqualification. As in the Wieman decision, the court ruled that the state could not classify innocent membership with knowing membership. The court added that the state must prove a particular member's intent to further the presumed unlawful aims of the organization.[3]

The Wieman, Shelton, and Keyishian decisions protect teachers' rights to join and participate in groups that may be unpopular with school officials or the community. They cut the ground from under efforts to limit teachers' group activities through guilt-by-association methods.

Federal courts have explicitly extended freedom of association to the right to join a teachers' union. A Seventh Circuit appeals court made this clear in a 1968 decision, *McLaughlin v. Tilendis.*[4] McLaughlin was an untenured teacher who claimed he had been fired because of his union activities. The district court that first heard the case ruled against McLaughlin, saying that a union could jeopardize the ability of the school to function. In reversing the lower court, the appeals court noted that the state did not outlaw unions and that school officials had not accused McLaughlin of engaging in illegal or disruptive acts. Even if the record had shown that the union had committed illegal acts, McLaughlin's union membership *per se* would not justify charging him with the misdeeds of the organization. If McLaughlin had, in fact, been fired for belonging to the union, school officials had violated his civil rights and were liable for damages.

Associational rights are not limited to affiliation. Teachers can work for a group, speak for it, or even work to supplant it with another group.

Greminger v. Seaborne[5]

Ron Greminger was president of the Community Teachers Association, a long-time affiliate of the Missouri State Teachers Association. When the school board denied teachers a salary increase, Greminger sought the assistance of a rival group, the Missouri National Education Association (MNEA). The school board members considered the MNEA a radical union-oriented group and a disruptive force. They refused to renew Greminger's contract.

> *A district court jury found that the board had violated Greminger's First Amendment rights. In affirming the decision, the U.S. Court of Appeals found that, although there was some animosity among Greminger's colleagues because of the change in affiliation, there was no disruption of school operations or the educational process. Greminger did not harass other teachers or the board. Nor did he make statements that were deliberately false or reckless.*
>
> *Because school officials had violated Greminger's constitutional rights in disregard of settled, indisputable law, they were liable for damages.*

Freedom of Speech

Teachers have the right to free speech. Protected speech includes school-related statements that are critical of the school administration and speech related to organizing fellow teachers. The free-speech right also extends to speech that is not related to school affairs. Comments about controversial political or social issues, both on and off school grounds, are protected.

Speaking Out on School Issues

Pickering v. Board of Education, a 1968 U.S. Supreme Court decision, is the foremost teacher's rights decision. It is nothing less than the teacher's Magna Charta.

> ### *Pickering v. Board of Education*[6]
> *Marvin Pickering was a teacher in and resident of the Lockport, Illinois, school district. He was upset by what he thought was duplicity in efforts by school officials to sell a bond issue. He wrote a long, rambling letter to the local newspaper that virtually accused the administration of lying about numerous aspects of its budget and building plans. The letter was scathing. It portrayed the administration as a gang of scoundrels.*
>
> *The school board dismissed Pickering for making false statements and impugning the integrity and competence of the board and school administration. His actions, they said, were "detrimental to the efficient operation and administration of the schools."*
>
> *Illinois courts upheld Pickering's dismissal. The Illinois Supreme Court ruled that (1) teachers do not share the citizen's right to criticize public officials; (2) Pickering's acceptance of a teaching position obliged him to refrain from speaking about the schools in any way that did not promote*

the interests of the schools; and (3) it was the responsibility of the school board to identify these interests. There was, however, a strong dissent, which managed to highlight the miscarriage of freedom. The U.S. Supreme Court finally overruled the Illinois majority.

The Supreme Court decision, delivered by Justice Thurgood Marshall, held conclusively that teachers do share with citizens the right to speak out on public issues. If a teacher's statements are substantially accurate, they provide no grounds for dismissal unless school officials can prove they caused disruption. Even if the statements are inaccurate, a showing of disruption is still required unless school officials can prove that the statements were knowingly false or reckless.

The Pickering case dealt with disruption in a narrow context. Marshall said that Pickering's comments were not disruptive because he did not criticize his immediate supervisors but instead criticized people with whom he had no normal daily contact.

The disruption aspect was later clarified by the Supreme Court in the Tinker case and subsequent decisions.[8] In *Tinker v. Des Moines,* the court said that disruption had to be real and substantial; mere apprehension of disruption or desire on the part of school authorities to avoid discomfort is not enough to overcome the right to free speech. Expressive activity cannot be proscribed or punished unless it "materially disrupts classwork or involves substantial disorder." Tinker has become the standard for the courts in teacher speech cases.

Not all expression by a public employee is constitutionally protected. The determination of what speech is protected involves balancing the rights of the teacher, as a citizen, in commenting on matters of public policy against the interest of the state, as employer, in promoting the efficient operation of a public service—in this case, the schools. The Pickering case concerned criticism of public officials sent to a newspaper. Does the right to free speech extend to private communications of a public employee?

Free speech is a means of assuring that individuals will not be afraid to express their ideas before the community. Should it also protect a teacher who tries to press her opinions on her supervisors? A recent Supreme Court decision found that it does:

Givhan v. Western Line Consolidated School District[9]
Western Line Consolidated District, a rural Mississippi

*school system, was integrated by order of the federal courts.
Bessie Givhan, a black teacher, was critical of the school
administration's racial policies and practices. The principal
charged that she displayed an insulting and hostile attitude
towards the administration and that she made petty and
unreasonable demands. After Givhan was dismissed, she
claimed discrimination and violation of her freedom of
speech.*

*After two days of testimony, the district court ruled in
favor of Givhan. Givhan's criticism was not constant, the
court said; the principal could identify only two specific
occasions. The criticisms were not petty; they dealt with
employment practices which Givhan thought were racially
discriminatory. The court concluded that the district had
fired Givhan to rid themselves of a critic of policies that were
conceivably discriminatory. Her dismissal was a violation of
the First Amendment.*

*The Fifth Circuit Court of Appeals reversed the deci-
sion. Givhan, it said, was a public employee who had
privately voiced complaints and expressed opinions to her
immediate superior. The purpose of the free-speech right, the
court said, was to permit public employees to inform the
community, not single out a supervisor to serve as an audience for privately expressed views. Thus, the court would
effectively remove constitutional protection from any teacher
who tried to go through channels to correct an inequitable
situation.*

*The U.S. Supreme Court disagreed. Although previous
free-speech decisions had involved public criticism, this
factor was not crucial. The high court ruled that a teacher
who arranges to speak privately with a supervisor rather than
express criticism publicly does not forfeit free-speech rights.*

The cases cited above suggest several of the limits on a teacher's
freedom of speech: A teacher's speech may not disrupt the school or
jeopardize working relationships. It may not be reckless or knowingly false. It must deal with issues of a public nature, not merely
address personal problems. Two other court decisions further illustrate the limitations on free speech:

Amburgey v. Cassady[10]
*Grace Amburgey was a nontenured teacher working as a
librarian at the Rowan County High School in Moorhead,
Kentucky. She was dismissed. She challenged her dismissal
on free-speech grounds.*

The court said that the evidence presented at trial sup-

ported the following facts:

- *Amburgey had shoved the superintendent after a board meeting.*
- *She had told teachers and custodians, using profane language, that the principal and superintendent were unfit for their positions.*
- *She had threatened to shoot the superintendent and remarked that both the principal and superintendent ought to be killed.*

The judge noted that the First Amendment protects a teacher's right to criticize internal school operations. Abuse of this right, however, removes the teacher's protection. Society's acceptance of the risks inherent in allowing people to make statements of personal views does not extend to insulting and profane statements that do not touch on factual issues of public or private concern: "The First Amendment has never been a shield for intemperate personal vilification of another."

In deciding whom to employ, it was appropriate for the board to consider the disruptive effect of Amburgey's intemperate language.

Jones v. Battle[11]

Jones, a probationary teacher, attended an open meeting of the school board. He told the board that he was not happy with his placement, and he questioned the integrity of his supervisors. He called one a "liar." The board dismissed Jones.

The judge who heard the dismissal appeal characterized Jones's comments as violently abusive and personally defamatory: "To publicly label and indelibly brand an administrative officer to his employer with such personal invective goes beyond the permissive limits." In upholding the dismissal, the judge also noted that (1) the superintendent had investigated Jones's charges and found them baseless; (2) Jones's charges could have revived previous racial problems and disruptions in the school; and (3) there was no likelihood of any future amiable professional relationship.

Amburgey and Jones crossed the boundary lines of free speech. Their comments were reckless, incendiary, personal, and false. Nevertheless, the courts understand that it is not always easy for a teacher to identify these boundaries, and they have been particularly sensitive to the problems of teachers involved in labor negotiations. For example, in *Roberts v. Lake Central School Corporation* the court heard the case of a teacher who had been fired for telling a meeting of teachers that the school administration was trying to buy them off with little items at the expense of big items. The court said that such statements represented the typical rhetoric of a negotiator and that the administration had been oversensitive. The statements were not so critical as to cause disruption.[12]

A second case, *Puentes v. Board,* dealt with the president of a teachers' union who had written a letter criticizing school officials. He was subsequently dismissed for unbecoming conduct and insubordination. The court ruled that he had been denied freedom of speech. The letter, the court said, was strident and excessive, but no worse. Although the letter contained factual inaccuracies, these were based on observations not accessible to the teacher and, therefore, not slanderous. Further, the letter caused no deleterious effects within the school system.[13]

Speech is only one of the school-related expressive activities protected by the First Amendment. It also protects petition and written communication between teachers.

Downs v. Conway School District[14]

The superintendent of the Conway School District had allowed an open incinerator near a school play area. When Mrs. Downs, a teacher, complained about the irritating smoke and the hazardous conditions for children, the superintendent told her that no one else had complained. So Mrs. Downs surveyed other teachers, by writing personal notes. The superintendent, stung by the teacher's action, told her that her contract would not be renewed. The court defended the teacher's right to petition and denounced the superintendent as an authoritarian incompetent.

In a second petition case, the Los Angeles City Board of Education tried to prevent teachers from circulating a petition in opposition to a funding cutback. The California Supreme Court ruled that the school was the most effective place for teachers to communicate with each other. Furthermore, "government has no interest in preventing the sort of disharmony which results inevitably from the mere expression of controversial ideas." The school board cannot demand that teachers refrain from criticizing policies or sharing ideas.[15]

Not only do teachers have the right to communicate, school officials cannot deny them the use of such facilities as mailboxes, lockers, and lounges. A federal district court overturned a New York school board's regulation which prohibited the use of faculty mailboxes for the distribution of literature.[16] The court said that the board had no absolute right to restrict the use of such facilities. The tension and turmoil incidental to collective bargaining were not sufficient justifications for prohibition; the board would have to demonstrate disruption or material interference with school activities.

Speaking Out on Political and Social Issues

While school-related issues are often a teacher's area of greatest concern, many teachers have also felt the need to express their views on broader political and social issues. Courts have supported the rights of teachers to adopt and express opinions on controversial issues *both in school and in the community.*

Speaking out in school. The public schools have a long tradition of limited involvement in social and political affairs. Schools are set apart—some would say isolated—as havens for contemplation. The governmental structure of education and the political independence, nonpartisan nature, and a political administration of school districts has enhanced this image of noninvolvement.

The Supreme Court's *Tinker v. Des Moines* decision rejected the proposition that the schools ought to be protected from the currents of public controversy and change. Justice Fortas wrote: "Students may not be regarded as closed-circuit recipients of only what the state chooses to communicate. They may not be confined to the expression of those sentiments that are officially approved."[17] Adopting Justice Brennan's language in the Keyishian free-association case, Justice Fortas reiterated that the classroom was peculiarly the "marketplace of ideas" and that the nation's future depends on leaders identified through "wide exposure to the robust exchange of ideas which discover truth but of a multitude of tongues, rather than through any kind of authoritative selection."

Teachers have the right to take positions on political or social issues and to express their opinions in school. Furthermore, school authorities cannot force teachers to take positions or participate in activities that conflict with their convictions. However, the right to have and express opinions is distinguishable from the freedom to advocate, proselytize for, or set up an alternative to the approved curriculum. In the classroom, a teacher must strive to present alternative perspectives fairly rather than to sell a particular perspective.

The classroom is supposed to be a marketplace, not a monopoly.

The teaching profession is committed to political neutrality. Practically all teachers believe that in the classroom they should adopt a pose of neutrality and nonpartisanship. They believe that to do otherwise would be irresponsible. However, there have been instances when teachers felt they could not in good conscience avoid expressing their true feelings about particular issues.

James v. Board[19]

Charles James, a teacher in upstate New York, wore an armband to school on Moratorium Day to protest the Vietnam War. He was dismissed.

In his order to reinstate James, Judge Irving Kaufman of the U.S. Court of Appeals noted several points in James's favor. First, citing the Tinker decision, he observed that teachers' speech should not be more restricted than students' speech. Second, although a teacher may have a more-pervasive influence on students than other students have, James had not proselytized or attempted to persuade his students that his values ought to be their values. Third, the students were sufficiently mature—16 or 17—to view the armband as a benign symbolic expression of the teacher's personal views. Finally, there was no disruption.

Russo v. Central School District No. 1[20]

The day at Sperry High School began with the Pledge of Allegiance and a salute to the flag. Everyone rose and saluted as the pledge was read over the intercom system—everyone except Susan Russo, a probationary teacher.

Russo believed that the phrase "liberty and justice for all" was empty and that to mouth the words was hypocrisy. Although she stood up with her home-room students and faced the flag, she neither pledged nor saluted. A second home-room teacher did, however, lead the students in the ritual.

School officials did not become aware of Russo's lapse for many months. At the end of the year, they did not renew her contract. She sued for violation of her free-speech rights.

In court, school officials gave six reasons to justify Russo's nonrenewal. The judge dismissed these as "trimmings to cloak the conduct of the board." The real issue, he said, was "whether a teacher could be discharged on the sole ground of her refusal to comply with a school regulation which required her to participate with her class in the Pledge of Allegiance."

The answer was no. The Supreme Court had already

decided, in West Virginia v. Barnett, *that students could not be compelled to say the pledge.*[21] *In the absence of disruption or efforts to proselytize, Russo's behavior was protected.*

Although a teacher has the right to refuse to participate, the court said that the state and school board have a substantial interest in flag salute programs: "It is a proper and appropriate function of our educational system to instill in young minds a healthy respect for the symbols of our national government." However, regulations designed to achieve this goal must be drawn so as not to sap the vitality of First Amendment freedoms.

The court ordered the board to reinstate Russo.

James and Russo had particular political commitments which they brought with them into the school. In both cases, the commitments were expressed symbolically; the teachers did not disrupt the school program or seek converts among the students. Teachers are not, however, limited to symbolic expressions of their commitments. They may prepare or sign petitions.[22] They may distribute political literature.[23] They may also tell students how they feel about issues.

Moore v. Gaston County Board of Education[24]

George Moore III was student-teaching in the Gaston County (North Carolina) schools. One day he substituted for a seventh-grade teacher. All went well until the afternoon class in the history of Africa, Asia, and the Middle East.

The students told Moore that the assignment concerned the development of religions in the Middle East. They were not prepared to recite, so he gave them 15 minutes to read the relevant seven pages. Moore's efforts to encourage discussions were, nevertheless, stymied until, following the text, he asked the students about the evolution of Hebraic beliefs.

The word "evolution" struck a nerve. A student asked Moore if he believed that humans had descended from monkeys. Moore responded that evolution was a valid theory. Another student asked if Moore believed that Adam and Eve were the first people. He answered that he thought that the story was symbolic of the unity of mankind and not to be taken literally. In response to additional questions, Moore revealed that he did not attend church, did not know what a "soul" was, and did not believe in life after death, heaven, or hell.

The next day, school authorities gave Moore his walking papers. In court, they accused him of teaching his own religion to a captive audience, lacking rapport with students, and attacking and ridiculing the students' beliefs. The judge,

> *however, concluded that Moore had been discharged for dis-*
> *cussing taboo matters in an unaccustomed manner. The*
> *judge said, "The inference fairly arises that if his responses*
> *had conformed to the locally accepted dogma, he would not*
> *have been discharged."*
>
> *The judge ruled that the school had violated Moore's*
> *First Amendment free-speech rights. By summarily terminat-*
> *ing his student-teaching assignment without a hearing, they*
> *also violated his right to due process and equal protection of*
> *the laws. In addition, by discharging Moore for his*
> *comments on Darwinian theory and biblical beliefs, school*
> *officials violated the establishment-of-religion clause.*

Teachers may bring their personal political and social commitments into the classroom. However, they should exercise restraint.
Teachers must not attempt to impose their beliefs on their students.
They must not interfere with the curriculum. They must not defy
reasonable requests of supervisors. And they must not disrupt the
school.

Birdwell v. Hazelwood School District[25]

> *Beauregard Birdwell, an algebra teacher at Hazelwood*
> *High School in Missouri, was dismissed in the middle of the*
> *contract year for disruption of the orderly and disciplined*
> *operation of the school. He appealed his dismissal.*
>
> *The activities that caused him to be fired began when it*
> *was announced that military recruiters would be on campus.*
> *Birdwell thought that the principal should first have con-*
> *sulted teachers and students. He told his students that they*
> *were 4,000 strong and that military visitors would not be*
> *tolerated by students at a nearby university. The court said*
> *that these statements were "infused with the spirit of violent*
> *action." Later, Birdwell confronted the military personnel in*
> *the school hallway and told them that they were not wanted.*
> *The court labeled this an "overt attempt to sabotage the*
> *visitation program by either disrupting the smooth operation*
> *of the program or by attempting to induce the military per-*
> *sonnel to leave the school premises." The court concluded*
> *that Birdwell's actions were designed not to further the*
> *marketplace of ideas, but to limit competition. In addition,*
> *he had put himself in the position of policymaker and*
> *enforcer in opposition to established school policies.*

La Rocca v. Rye City School District[26]

> *Joan La Rocca was dedicated to the tenets of an obscure*
> *religious organization. She was dismissed from her teaching*

job after a hearing panel concluded that she had proselytized students to attend the organization's meetings. La Rocca had preached her religion's beliefs under the guise of offering students guidance. She had used her authority as a teacher to recruit students. She had used her office for prayer sessions. She had disobeyed her principal's order to stop proselytizing. The panel concluded that her use of school hours and property for these purposes suggested that the public school was proselytizing in violation of separation of church and state.

La Rocca appealed to the courts for review of her dismissal. The court ruled that the record showed substantial evidence that she had violated the establishment-of-religion clause and the state constitution, which prohibits the use of state property for religious purposes. Dismissal was not disproportionate to the offense, especially since La Rocca told the hearing panel she did not feel required to abide by the principal's directive to cease proselytizing.

Speaking out in the community. It follows logically that if teachers are protected when they express controversial opinions in school, they are also protected when they speak in the community. Neither school officials nor concerned citizens may take advantage of the teacher's position as a public employee to stifle free expression. A quick review of four decisions illustrates how the courts have protected teachers from retribution for their expressive activities outside school.

In *Jervey v. Martin* (1972), a teacher at a junior college wrote a letter to *Redbook* magazine praising an article on premarital sexual relations and saying he planned to use it in his class. He was discharged by the school but reinstated by the court.[27] While school officials have a say in what enters the classroom, they have no authority to regulate a teacher's opinions.

In *Montgomery v. White* (1969), a Texas teacher challenged the school board's ban on all political activity other than voting. The U.S. District Court overruled the ban on the grounds that it stifled personal liberty and threatened popular government.[28]

In *Johnson v. Branch* (1966), the contract of a black teacher active in civil rights in the community was not renewed. Knowing that the civil rights activity was protected, the school board gave other reasons for firing the teacher. After examining the stated reasons for dismissal, the U.S. Court of Appeals said they were so trivial as to render the nonrenewal arbitrary and capricious.[29]

Finally, in *Woodward v. Hereford Independent School District* (1976), the contract of a Texas English teacher who had already successfully completed six one-year contracts with the school district was not renewed. His nonrenewal followed shortly after he had been elected president of the local American Civil Liberties Union (ACLU). Reviewing the facts, the court concluded that only the ACLU activities were involved; nothing else of consequence was mentioned by school authorities. Since Woodward's activities were protected by the First and Fourteenth Amendments, he was reinstated.[30]

Tenure and the First Amendment

How does tenure affect free speech and association rights? What if the position is only part time or temporary?

Tenure or full-time status are not relevant to the possession of First Amendment rights. Nobody—probationary, part-time, or tenured—can be fired, nonrenewed or punished in any other way by a public school for asserting their constitutional rights. The Supreme Court stated this clearly in *Perry v. Sindermann:*

> For at least a quarter-century, this court has made clear that even though a person has no "right" to a valuable governmental benefit and even though the government may deny him the benefit for any number of reasons, there are some reasons upon which the government may not rely. It may not deny a benefit to a person on a basis that infringes on his constitutionally protected interests. . . . Thus the respondent's lack of a contractual or tenure "right" to reemployment . . . is immaterial to his free-speech claim.[31]

Many of the cases discussed in this chapter have involved non-tenured teachers, among them Keyishian, Shelton, McLaughlin, Greminger, and Russo. Moore was a student teacher. All prevailed, the status of each notwithstanding.

How Teachers Can Protect Their Rights

Freedom of association, speech, and petition are teachers' rights. However they are not handed to teachers on a silver platter. Teachers must understand their rights, claim their rights, and sometimes go to court to defend their rights. Teachers who feel that school authorities are violating their constitutional rights can go to the federal courts and sue for various types of relief, including an injunction to prevent further interference, reinstatement if the teacher has been transferred or fired, and damages if the teacher's reputation has been hurt.

The federal courts have procedures for adjudicating dismissals or other school-imposed sanctions when teachers allege that their constitutional rights have been violated.[32] The initial burden of proof is on the teacher—to show that the decision was actually based on the school board's disapproval of the exercise of constitutionally protected rights. The teacher must prove that the exercise of rights was constitutionally protected and it was a substantial or motivating factor in the school board's decision. If the teacher can prove these allegations, the school board must demonstrate by a preponderance of evidence that it would have reached the same decision without regard to the protected conduct. The federal district court hears the evidence and determines the true reasons for dismissal.

There is no question that the need for a teacher to prove that constitutionally protected activities were a direct cause of punishment is a demanding requirement. However, it is designed to protect both teachers and school authorities. The courts generally can be counted on to support the exercise of protected rights. But they cannot allow a First Amendment defense to shield incompetence or other justifiable grounds for teacher dismissal.

For example, in *Doyle v. Mt. Healthy,* Doyle claimed he was not renewed because of his union activities and because of a phone call to a local radio station in which he complained about a faculty dress code.[33] The school board claimed he was not renewed because of his "immaturity" and "lack of tact," as exhibited in both the radio station call *and other incidents.* The "other incidents" included publicly arguing with a cafeteria worker and a teacher, calling students "SOBs," and making a rude gesture at some unruly coeds. The question was: Was Doyle dismissed because he exercised constitutionally protected rights, or would he have been dismissed anyway?

Once the teacher has shown that punishment was a direct result of the exercise of protected freedoms, the only defense available to school authorities is to show that the teacher's activities resulted in *disruption.* As the Supreme Court has emphasized since the Tinker decision, authorities can limit expressive or associational activity only if it "materially disrupts classwork or involves substantial disorder or invasion of the rights of others."[34]

A teacher whose rights have been violated by public officials is entitled to reinstatement and damages. School authorities have tried to claim that they are immune—that they cannot be sued for damages. They are not immune. Supervisors who violate the rights of subordinates are personally liable for damages. Local governing bodies may be held liable if official action is determined to be responsible for deprivation of rights protected by the constitution.[35]

Under the federal supremacy clause, federal courts have rejected school governments' claims to absolute immunity under common law, sovereign immunity, or statutory immunity. As the court noted in the McLaughlin union-membership case, school administrators "retain only qualified immunity, dependent on good-faith action. . . . At best, defendants' qualified immunity in this case means that they can prevail only if they show that the plaintiffs were discharged on justifiable grounds."[36] The constitutional right to association is so well established that the McLaughlin court did not even suggest the possibility of a defense based on good-faith ignorance of protected rights.

More recently, in a student rights decision *(Wood v. Strickland,* 1975), the Supreme Court attempted to clarify the limits of school government immunity. School officials should understand that actions taken in good-faith fulfillment of their responsibilities and within the bounds of reason will not be punished. The standard is that an official "must be acting sincerely and in the belief that he is doing right, but an act violating a student's constitutional rights can be no more justified by ignorance or disregard of settled, indisputable law . . . than by the presence of actual malice. . . . [A] school board member . . . must be held to a standard of conduct based not only on permissible intentions, but also on knowledge of the basic, unquestioned constitutional rights of his charges."[37]

A teacher's rights to associate, assemble, speak, and petition are basic and unquestioned. The Supreme Court has been consistent and steadfast in affirming these rights. Responsible officials, school administrators, and supervisors cannot plead good-faith ignorance when called to account for violating them.

Notes to Chapter 7

1. *Wieman v. Updegraff,* 344 U.S. 183 (1953).

2. *Shelton v. Tucker,* 364 U.S. 479 (1960).

3. *Keyishian v. New York Board of Regents,* 385 U.S. 589 (1967).

4. *McLaughlin v. Tilendis,* 389 F. 2d 287 (7th Cir., 1968).

5. *Greminger v. Seaborne,* 584 F. 2d 275 (8th Cir., 1978).

6. *Pickering v. Board of Education,* 391 U.S. 563 (1968). Also see *Zoll v. Eastern Alamakee Community School District,* 588 F. 2d 246 (8th Cir., 1978). Rose Zoll, an Alamakee County teacher for 29 years, was fired after she wrote two letters to the editor of the local newspaper which sharply criticized her school's administration. A district court jury found that the principal and superintendent were biased in their evaluation of her work in retaliation for her exercise of First Amendment rights. The principal and superintendent were assessed maximum damages. The board was ordered to reinstate Zoll.

   Sometimes the teacher cannot meet the burden of proof that retaliation for the exercise of protected rights led to dismissal; see *Gorham v. Jewett,* 392 F. Supp. 22 (D. Mass., 1975).

7. *Tinker v. Des Moines School District,* 393 U.S. 503, 509, 513 (1969).

8. *Grayned v. City of Rockford,* 408 U.S. 104 (1971).

9. *Givhan v. Western Line Consolidated School District,* 555 F. 2d 1309 (5th Cir., 1977); vacated, 439 U.S. 410 (1979). See also *McGill v. Board,* 602 F. 2d 774 (7th Cir., 1979). A jury found that Barbara McGill had been involuntarily transferred in retaliation for remarks she made in the teachers' lounge concerning a master contract. The district court ruled and the appellate court confirmed that the master collective bargaining contract was a subject of public concern and, therefore, her expression of opinion was protected.

10. *Amburgey v. Cassady,* 370 F. Supp. 571 (E.D. Ky., 1974). Other cases in which courts found that teachers had exceeded the boundaries of acceptable criticism include *Gilbertson v. McAlister,* 403 F. Supp. 1 (D. Conn., 1975) and *Palo Verde Unified School District v. Hensey,* 88 Cal. Rptr. 570 (App., 1970).

11. *Jones v. Battle,* 315 F. Supp. 601 (D. Conn., 1970).

12. *Roberts v. Lake Central School Corporation,* 317 F. Supp. 63 (N.D. Ind., 1970).

13. *Puentes v. Board,* 302 N.Y.S. 2d 824 (Ct. of App. of N.Y., 1969). For a different outcome, see *Moore v. Winfield City Board of Education,* 452 F. 2d 726 (5th Cir., 1971).

14. *Downs v. Conway School District,* 328 F. Supp. 338 (E.D. Ark., 1971).

15. *Los Angeles Teachers Union v. Board,* 455 P. 2d 827 (Supreme Ct. of Calif., 1979).

16. *Friedman v. Union Free School District No. 1,* 314 F. Supp. 223 (E.D. N.Y., 1970).

17. *Tinker v. Des Moines* at 511.

18. Ibid. at 512.

19. *James v. Board,* 461 F. 2d 566 (2nd Cir., 1972). See also *Cooper v. Ross,* 472 F. Supp. 802 (E.D. Ark., 1979). Grant Cooper, an associate professor of history, told his students that he was a Marxist and that his courses inevitably contained a Marxist perspective. The court ruled that protected activity was the motivating factor in the university's decision not to reappoint him and that Cooper was, therefore, entitled to reappointment.

20. *Russo v. Central School District No. 1,* 469 F. 2d 623 (2nd Cir., 1972). Cert. denied, 411 U.S. 932 (1973).

21. *West Virginia v. Barnett,* 319 U.S. 624 (1943).

22. *Petitions of John Davenport et al.,* 283 A. 2d 452 (Supreme Ct. of Vt., 1971).

23. See *Los Angeles Teachers Union v. Board* and *Friedman v. Union.*

24. *Moore v. Gaston County Board of Education,* 357 F. Supp. 1037 (W.D. N.C., 1973).

25. *Birdwell v. Hazelwood School District,* 352 F. Supp. 613 (E.D. Mo., 1972).

26. *La Rocca v. Rye City School District,* 406 N.Y.S. 2d 348 (A.D., 1978).

27. *Jervey v. Martin,* 336 F. Supp. 1350 (W.D. Va., 1972).

28. *Montgomery v. White,* 320 F. Supp. 303 (E.D. Tex., 1969).

29. *Johnson v. Branch,* 364 F. 2d 177 (4th Cir., 1966).

30. *Woodward v. Hereford Independent School District,* 421 F. Supp. 93 (N.D. Tex., 1976).

31. *Perry v. Sindermann,* 408 U.S. 593, 597 (1972).

32. The procedure was specified in *Doyle v. Mt. Healthy,* 429 U.S. 274 (1977); also see *Givhan v. Western* at 1314. Teachers are protected from any deprivation or sanction, including transfer; see *Adcock v. Board,* 109 Cal. Rptr. 676 (Supreme Ct., 1973) and *McGill v. Board.* RIF (see *Zoll v. Eastern)* and dismissal or nonrenewal are also covered.

33. *Doyle v. Mt. Healthy.*

34. *Tinker v. Des Moines* at 513.

35. In *Monell v. Dept. of Social Services of the City of New York,* 436 U.S. 658, 690 (1977), the court held that when official policy or acts representing official policy inflict injury, the government entity is responsible. More recently, in *Owen v. City of Independence,* Mo. _____ U.S. _____ 100 S. Ct. 1398 (1980), a majority of the Supreme Court held that governments could not claim immunity defenses (e.g., sovereign immunity, good-faith immunity, or immunity based on the performance of governmental or discretionary functions; see discussion in Chapter 3) when they violate citizens' civil rights.

36. *McLaughlin v. Tilendis* at 290.

37. *Wood v. Strickland,* 420 U.S. 308, 321 (1975).

8.
LIFE-STYLE CHOICES

What is "proper"? What is "socially acceptable"? What is legal? The answers to such questions changed dramatically during the 1960s and 1970s. The value of conformity declined. The value of individuality rose. "Alternative life styles" gained acceptance. People's hair styles, clothing, places of residence, and leisure-time activities became recognized as extensions of their personalities.

General tolerance for individual rights can be chronicled in terms of changes in laws restricting personal freedom.[1] Laws against birth control, abortion, pornography, and fornication were struck down. Laws against victimless crimes—prostitution, drug use, gambling, curfew violation, homosexual practices—were often enforced haphazardly. Laws that protected individuals from arbitrary search and seizure or police action were strengthened.

Laws also expanded individual rights. Young people gained the right to vote at age 18. Women were recognized as equal in employment, general civil status, and even school athletics. Older adults gained the right to keep their jobs rather than retire at 60, 62, or 65.

These changes in attitudes and laws have had considerable impact on the lives of teachers. In the not-so-good—and not-so-ancient—old days, communities took an active interest in the public and private lives of teachers.[2] A teacher's friends, visitors, socializing, dancing, drinking, worshiping, marrying, and parenting were all considered legitimate concerns of school authorities. Teachers were expected to consume inconspicuously and to refrain from offending local business interests. They were expected to be nonpolitical and nonpartisan. A teacher's political energies were expected to be channeled into such neutral civic affairs as the Community Chest, the Girl Scouts, and the YMCA. Even the League of Women Voters was considered somewhat suspect.

Today, teachers can have private lives, and they can make significant choices in their life styles. Local boards, local administrators, and local busybodies cannot investigate or regulate every phase of a teacher's existence.

This is not to say that there are no limits on a teacher's personal freedom; some legitimate demands associated with the job have been recognized by the courts. The school system, as an employer, can require its agents or representatives to present themselves in a way that enhances the image of the school. The state or school system, as a representative of the public, may require public employees to conform to certain rules or regulations as a condition of employment. The public may reasonably expect teachers to conform to particular moral or sociocultural standards as a condition for entrusting minor children to the care of the school.

What are the limits to teachers' rights to pursue their own life styles? Two issues are relevant: (1) How does a given behavior affect students, coworkers, or the school? (2) How important is the behavior or activity to the teacher's sense of self?

A teacher's personal behavior may have positive or negative effects on students, colleagues, or the school, or it may have no effect. Courts have held that teachers' activities can be constrained legitimately if they threaten to harm students or jeopardize education through their harmful effects on collegial or supervisory relationships. Benign behavior is acceptable; harmful behavior is not.

It is the responsibility of the local board of education to determine what is harmful. This is part of the board's representative responsibility. Courts have given boards wide latitude and discretion in deciding whether a teacher's activities are harmful. However, their judgments and actions cannot be arbitrary or capricious. A school board must demonstrate that its determination is the result of a reasoned process and that there is evidence to support its belief that a teacher's behavior is harmful to the school. This does not mean that school officials must poll the students or faculty. The professional judgments of people with appropriate experience and information form an adequate basis for making such a determination.

It is not always easy to know what is harmful. There are varying degrees of harm. A teacher's activities may be more harmful or less harmful to a school. Therefore, a second consideration—the teacher's right to privacy—is used to balance the consideration of potential harm. The following questions must be asked: Is the harm so great that no interest of the teacher can justify the teacher's activity? Or is the teacher's interest in the activity so important to his or her sense of self that the school ought to adjust to it?

Courts have tried to determine what is important to the individual by distinguishing between the "private person" and the "public person."

The public person is the individual as presented to others. The public person is the sum total of an individual's grooming, dress, style of dealing with others, public statements, and public actions. It is the manipulable self.

The private self is the core person, with a unique combination of values, behavior, goals, relationships, and needs.

The private person is protected by custom and law. Acts and commitments that are kept to oneself are of no concern to society. However, society, institutions, and individuals do make decisions about which acts are truly private and which acts are public. In general, sexual behavior, marriage, procreation, family life, child rearing, and religion fall within a "zone of privacy" that has gained constitutional protection.[3] They are private because they are the subject of intimate decision making and because they do not affect others adversely (and thus are none of their business). Governments have no legitimate interest in these private affairs, and the individual has the right to be left alone.

The public person enjoys fewer protections. Because changes in the public person have less bearing on individual identity, it may be reasonable to expect people to comply with certain kinds of norms. Some aspects of the public person—dress, hair style, manner of speaking—may have so little adverse effect on others that no effort will be made to change them. However, a teacher's pattern of interaction with students, colleagues, and parents is both public and important. Similarly, public immorality and lawbreaking are both harmful and public and, therefore, are legitimate concerns of government.

Although society recognizes some areas of life as private, individuals may forfeit their right to privacy. Some people feel a need to crusade for their life-style choice. Others are exhibitionists who flaunt their controversial life styles. Still others focus public attention on their private lives by misbehavior or indiscretion. Some live in such tightly knit communities that discretion is not a real option. The right to privacy can be lost by intention or by indiscretion.

By contrast, individuals may claim their right to privacy if behavior that first seems to be a matter of "mere appearance" can be shown to be part of their private selves. Symbols of racial and religious identity may meet this criterion. The head covering of a Jew or a Sikh, a black man's Afro haircut, or an American Indian's long hair may symbolize deeply held commitments.

Teachers have the greatest protection when their behavior is private and does not affect the schools. As behavior moves from private to public in context and from benign to harmful in effect, school authorities can exercise more control over the teacher. Schools can exercise the greatest authority over teachers whose behavior is both harmful and public. In such circumstances, teachers have little protection.

The dimensions of teachers' life-style freedom may be clarified by examining seven areas: appearance, sexual behavior, marriage and pregnancy, retirement age, crime, alcohol and drugs, and residency.

Appearance

School authorities may make and enforce reasonable regulations governing a teacher's dress and appearance. Arguments about the definition of "reasonable" have filled arbitration sessions and courts.

Why do school boards and administrations want to regulate the appearance of teachers? Three arguments are common: First, the teacher sets the tone for the classroom. A teacher whose appearance is sloppy or unconventional or tasteless is setting an inappropriate tone. Second, the teacher represents the school and the teaching profession to the public. Appropriate professional dress can enhance the image of the profession and increase respect for the school; inappropriate dress can provoke negative assessments. Third, it is easier to enforce student dress codes if teachers adhere to comparable rules.

Teachers have used both academic freedom and the right to privacy as arguments against dress regulations.

The core of the academic-freedom argument is that a teacher's appearance is a form of communication which is protected under freedom of speech. The courts have rejected this line of reasoning on two grounds: first, that the academic freedom of public school teachers is, itself, restricted—school authorities *can* regulate a teacher's speech; second, that dress is not "pure speech" but, rather, an educational method that a teacher uses to influence student response. Thus, a disagreement between a teacher and an administrator or school board about dress is a disagreement about educational methods. The teacher's opinion is entitled to no greater consideration than that of the school board and its administrators. Because the court is not in a position to judge among educational methods, decisions about appropriate dress should be made by those to whom the legislature and the people have given administrative authority.

The reasoning on the basis of privacy is more complex. Generally, court decisions have been congruent with the theory of teacher freedom.

The courts have held that the state, as an employer, may have a legitimate interest in regulating and restricting the rights of employees. They have rejected challenges to that legitimate interest. A policeman's challenge to hair-style regulations was rejected by the U.S. Supreme Court as "trivial"; the majority decision in *Kelly v. Johnson* said that hair-style regulations implicated "only the more general contours" of protected constitutional rights.[4] The only constitutional issue raised by hair-style regulations is whether the regulation is so irrational that it may be branded arbitrary. Any reason for the regulation is reason enough. The rights to privacy and liberty are available to protect personal decisions more basic than those involving hair style.

The courts have used this line of reasoning to reject the arguments of several teachers who have wanted to dress in nonconforming styles. In *Miller v. School District,* the court upheld an Illinois school's dress and grooming regulations against a teacher who claimed he had a right to appear as he wished.[5] In *Tardif v. Quinn,* the court upheld the dismissal of a Massachusetts teacher who wore very short skirts.[6] In *East Hartford Education Association v. School District,* a Connecticut court upheld the school board's right to require male teachers to wear ties.[7]

One form of nonconforming dress that has been protected is religious garb. At least two state courts and one state legislature have upheld the right of teachers to wear religious dress. In *Rawlings v. Butler,* the Court of Appeals of Kentucky held, "the dress and emblems worn by Sisters (of the Roman Catholic church) do not deprive them of their right to teach in public schools."[8] And in *Moore v. Board of Education,* an Ohio court ruled that, in the absence of statute or regulation, "religious garb may be worn by teachers in teaching in public schools."[9] The Arkansas legislature has passed a law that specifically recognizes the right of teachers to wear religious garb: "Hereafter, any teacher may wear the clothing of any established and recognized religion in the public schools. . . ."[10]

Religious dress is not, however, protected in all states. Oregon law specifically prohibits wearing such clothing: "No teacher in any public school shall wear any religious dress while engaged in his duties as a teacher."[11] A similar statute exists in North Dakota. Where such statutes exist, they have been upheld in state courts.

Other aspects of appearance have also been protected in court decisions. Courts have ruled, for example, that facial hair is not a trivial aspect of appearance. Unlike clothes, a beard cannot be put on and taken off at will, nor can it be temporarily covered during school hours. Because facial hair is not a trivial aspect of appearance, rules about it must meet a higher standard than rules about clothing. Courts have defined that standard as *a reasoned belief that failure to enforce the regulation* (against nontrivial aspects of appearance) *would harm the school.* If harm cannot be established, the rule cannot remain; privacy and liberty interests prevail. Generally, school authorities have not been able to demonstrate that a beard on a teacher creates a harmful effect.

Two cases on beards can be cited. In *Braxton v. Board,* a black teacher who was fired for growing a goatee argued that the goatee was an expression of heritage, culture, and racial pride. The court accepted his argument and ruled that his dismissal was illegal because it had been arbitrary, discriminatory, and racially motivated. The court noted that there was no personal-appearance regulation against wearing a beard and that no disruption had resulted from the beard.[12]

The absence of disruption or other evidence of harm is the critical component of a second case, *Finot v. Pasadena City Board of Education.* Finot was transferred from classroom teaching duties to less-desirable home teaching duties after he grew a beard. In his suit against the board, he claimed a liberty interest in the beard. The court ruled that, in the absence of evidence of harm to the school, Finot's transfer was arbitrary and could not stand.[13]

Obesity has also been protected as a nontrivial aspect of appearance. An applicant for a substitute teacher's license in New York was rejected on the grounds of obesity. She sued; the court said that a rule against hiring fat people was arbitrary and capricious.[14] Similarly, another district was told that it could not refuse to renew the contract of a physical education teacher simply because she was overweight. The court rejected the arguments that the teacher was not a "model of health and vigor" and that she might have trouble demonstrating or teaching certain aspects of physical education. It ruled that in the absence of evidence of specific harm to students or the school, the teacher could not be terminated because of her appearance.[15]

Sexual Behavior

A teacher's private life is protected. A teacher's adherence to conventional behavior in public is expected. Deviations from the norm are noticed.

Some curiosity about the sex lives of teachers is unavoidable. Sexual behavior is at the core of "morality" for many people. Parents and other citizens may be legitimately concerned about the moral standards of those who teach.

Until recently, schools have been viewed as islands set apart from the real world. The island protected students from the harsh realities of life, work, and sex. School authorities and their most vociferous clientele groups have preferred to maintain the image of traditional family morality despite widespread evidence of divorce, teen pregnancies, and promiscuity.

Courts have tended to endorse this holier-than-thou stance. Some judges have believed that the schools are the best hope for the future. Others have simply felt that school boards, representing conventional community morality, have the right and the duty to promote this morality in the community's schools.

"Conventional sexual behavior" consists of a husband and wife engaging in intimate sexual relations within the privacy of their home. Public disclosure that a woman is sleeping with her husband cannot harm the students or the school. On the other hand, disclosures about partner swapping, adultery, premarital intimacy, homosexual relationships, and other unconventional sexual behavior are seen as potentially harmful.

It does not follow that school authorities are free to fire any teacher who is involved in an unconventional sexual relationship. The courts have recognized changes in prevailing attitudes and behavior; they have conceded that sexual relations outside marriage do not compromise the moral integrity of the teacher. The standard recognized by the courts is that of harm to students or school.

There can be no evidence that the students or the school have been harmed as long as sexual behavior remains private and personal. However, any disclosure can diminish a teacher's right to privacy. Teachers who intentionally expose their private lives to public view forfeit their right to privacy. The same is true if they expose their private behavior indirectly. If others expose a teacher's private behavior, their motives for doing so are relevant. Courts have supported teachers whose isolated incidents of misconduct were exposed for malicious motives.

Erb v. Iowa State Board of Public Instruction[16]
Richard Erb was caught in an adulterous relationship with another man's wife. His own wife forgave him, and his neighbors and friends seemed willing to forget about the incident. His employer, the local school district, renewed his contract. The Iowa State Board of Instruction, however, revoked his teaching certificate, calling him "morally unfit." Erb sued to get his certificate back. The court ruled that there was not sufficient evidence to find Erb unfit to teach in Iowa. The incident was an isolated one; the circumstances were unlikely to occur again. There was no evidence of harm to the school or the community.

Reinhardt v. Board of Education[17]
Elizabeth Reinhardt, a tenured teacher, had been married for less than a month when she requested maternity leave. Her child was due soon.
The board asked her to resign. When she refused, they fired her for immorality.
Reinhardt sued the board. An Illinois appeals court ruled that her dismissal was illegal because there was no evidence of harm to students, colleagues, or the school.

Fisher v. Snyder[18]
The board of education fired Frances Fisher because "men not related to her" stayed at her apartment. How did the board know this? A door-to-door sales representative,

> *who happened to be the wife of a local minister, paid a surprise call on the teacher one Saturday morning. She reported her "findings" to the board.*
>
> *Mrs. Fisher's case against dismissal was argued in a federal district court. She claimed violations of her rights to association and privacy. The court ruled that her rights had been violated and that there was no evidence of any impropriety that had bearing on any interest of the school board. There was no proof of harm to students or the school.*

The Erb, Reinhardt, and Fisher cases suggest some of the boundaries of the teacher's zone of privacy. Sometimes the zone is constricted.

> ### *Sullivan v. Meade Independent School District*[19]
> *Kathleen Sullivan, a transplanted New Yorker, taught elementary school in Union Center, South Dakota. She lived in a mobile home that the district provided. One day, her boyfriend also moved in.*
>
> *The arrangement became known quickly. Parents complained to the school board about it. School authorities told Sullivan that they would dismiss her if her boyfriend did not leave.*
>
> *The boyfriend stayed. The board fired Sullivan. She sued to retain her position.*
>
> *The U.S. district court ruled against Sullivan. It held that the teacher's character and integrity were legitimate concerns of her employer. It also said that her living arrangement was related to the educational process. The small community in which she taught was offended. Sullivan had disregarded local norms. There was a potential of harm to students and the school.*

There is an interesting contrast to the Fisher case in *Acanfora v. Montgomery Board of Education.*[20] Acanfora was a homosexual. The Pennsylvania Department of Education knew this when he was granted a teaching certificate. The secretary of education announced that he was issuing the certificate "reluctantly"; he made the announcement at a televised news conference. As a result of the public disclosure, Acanfora was transferred to a nonteaching position. He protested the transfer, and he made a number of radio and television appearances to explain his position. The board dismissed him.

When the case went to court, the court found that the original transfer was arbitrary and unjustified: Acanfora had been discreet about his private life; his activities had been well within his rights of freedom of association.

Nevertheless, the court upheld his dismissal. In *Fisher v. Snyder,* the court was sympathetic to a teacher who had been victimized by a community busybody. In *Acanfora v. Montgomery,* the Court seemed to say that the teacher had been his own worst enemy. The court ruled that Acanfora's radio and television appearances exceeded the bounds of reasonable self-defense. In making such appearances, the teacher had shown indifference to the bounds of propriety. He was, furthermore, likely to bring harm to the school system. The court concluded that there was not only a *right* to privacy but a *duty* of privacy.

The determination that a particular kind of sexual behavior is harmful or that a teacher's right to privacy outweighs potential harm to a school is at best inexact. Thus, courts often feel obliged to give the benefit of the doubt to the reasoned judgments of school authorities.

Gaylord v. Tacoma School District No. 10[21]

James Gaylord had taught at Tacoma's Wilson High School for 12 years without incident. A former student who, on the basis of a private conversation, suspected that Gaylord was a homosexual reported his suspicion to the school assistant principal. Gaylord admitted his homosexuality to the assistant principal, and he was discharged for immorality.

The trial court concluded that when Gaylord's homosexual status became known it impaired his teaching efficiency. If he had not been fired, the result would have been fear, confusion, suspicion, and parental hostility to the school.

On appeal, the majority opinion of the Washington Supreme Court began by focusing on immorality as a cause for dismissal. Immorality, the court said, is not to be construed in its abstract sense apart from its effect upon teaching efficiency or fitness to teach. Is homosexuality immoral? Homosexuals do immoral and illegal things. Gaylord admitted his status as a homosexual. Although there was no evidence of overt acts of homosexuality, Gaylord did not deny committing overt acts typical of homosexuals. Thus, he was actively immoral while employed as a teacher. Furthermore, the majority said, homosexuality is widely condemned as immoral. A majority of people react negatively to homosexuals. Thus Gaylord's continued presence would harm the school.

The dissent argued first that there was no evidence that Gaylord had ever committed an illegal or immoral act. Mere proof of homosexual status is insufficient to justify a charge of immorality. The school district had the burden of proving that Gaylord was involved in an overt immoral or illegal act. Gaylord could not be expected to deny participation in acts which were never mentioned or described by the school board.

Second, the school district failed to establish that Gaylord's teaching was impaired by his homosexuality. Although he admitted that he had been a homosexual during the entire time he had taught at Wilson High, his homosexuality clearly had not impaired his teaching performance. Speculation on what effect Gaylord's homosexuality might have on his future performance in the classroom was conjecture. In the absence of any factual (as opposed to imagined) connection between Gaylord's homosexuality and his effectiveness as a teacher, the dismissal had violated his constitutional due-process rights.

Marriage and Pregnancy

For many years, the marriage of a female teacher was grounds for her dismissal. In a study of teacher contracts in the 1920s, William Anderson found that in 10 of 33 cities in his survey, a teacher's contract could be voided if she married.[22] In 1925 E.E. Lewis wrote, in *Personnel Problems of the Teaching Profession:*

A woman teacher's marriage is equivalent to resignation in the majority of American school districts. Where there are no formal regulations, the policy is often pursued of refusing to reappoint. Few school boards place married women on a par with the unmarried except when they are widowed, deserted, divorced, unencumbered with family duties, or need to make their own living.[23]

Although Anderson suggests that this practice was largely illegal at the time, courts were upholding dismissal for marriage at least as late as the 1950s.[24] Today, school authorities may no longer discriminate against married persons, and there appears to be little sentiment for doing so. Indeed, state laws that forbid discrimination on the basis of marriage seem like quaint reminders of bygone prejudices.

Rules about teacher pregnancy have similarly changed with the times. Only a short time ago, pregnant women were discouraged from participating in any activity, especially paid employment. School authorities favored early leaves of absence on the grounds of continuity of instruction, classroom control, and health and safety.

Marriage and pregnancy, like other areas of personal and family life, are protected by the due-process clause of the Fourteenth Amendment. The U.S. Supreme Court has held that because rules about marriage and pregnancy directly affect basic civil rights, due process requires that such rules must not needlessly, arbitrarily, or capriciously impinge upon people's lives. The question raised by such rules is whether they can be justified by the rulemakers.

In 1974, in *Cleveland Board of Education v. LaFleur,* the U.S. Supreme Court ruled that arbitrary and mandatory leaves of absence for pregnancy have no rational relationship to legitimate school interests. The Cleveland board had required teachers to leave their jobs after the fifth month of pregnancy. The court recognized the fact that women and pregnancies are not uniform; they endorsed the use of physicians' certificates to establish both the time for beginning a leave and the time for returning to work. The court did not specifically outlaw the use of uniform dates, but it did say that employers would have to meet the burden of proving that such policies were justified by the inability of the women to perform their jobs or by administrative necessity.[25]

DeLaurier v. San Diego Unified School District[26]

The San Diego School System required a pregnant teacher to take a leave of absence at the beginning of the ninth month of pregnancy. When the district enforced this policy on Karen DeLaurier, she sued to be allowed to work until the onset of labor.

The court analyzed the issue from two perspectives, Title VII (sex discrimination) and due process.

Because mandatory maternity leave imposes a substantial burden on women and not on men, it is on its face discriminatory. Thus, the employer must give some legitimate nondiscriminatory reason for its policy in order to defend against a charge of sex bias. The school district presented the following evidence: (1) it required the one-month leave in order to provide qualified substitutes and, thus, achieve its administrative and educational objectives and (2) the physical condition and abilities of a woman in her final month of pregnancy were sufficiently impaired so as to reduce her effectiveness. The court accepted this evidence as a sufficient defense to justify discrimination.

DeLaurier's due-process rights would have been violated if the board's policy had needlessly, arbitrarily, or capriciously impinged on her liberty right to bear a child or if the policy had unduly penalized her by not allowing her to show why the rule should not apply in her case. In Cleveland v. LaFleur, *the Supreme Court had ruled that requiring teachers to take leaves during the fifth month of pregnancy was arbitrary and a violation of due process. Here, however, the court said that the evidence of competent doctors and school administrators was sufficient to justify mandatory leave during the last few weeks of pregnancy. Furthermore, DeLaurier had not been denied equal protection because the district was able to show that the leave policy was rationally related to important governmental objectives.*

A strong dissenting opinion took issue with both of the majority's conclusions. The dissent argued, first, that mandatory maternity leave imposes a special burden on women. All other health-related leaves began and ended on dates chosen individually by teachers. The district enforced a uniform date only for pregnancy leaves.

Second, the dissent said, a district must show that discrimination is necessary to ensure the safe and efficient performance of a particular job. Thus, the district must show that the ninth month of pregnancy presents problems that are not presented by earlier stages of pregnancy or by other temporary disabilities. While it is always convenient for an employer to know when an employee will be absent, why should advance notification be required only for pregnancy? Why not also for elective surgery? Why couldn't notice be achieved by agreement between the individual teacher and the district? Given the small number of teachers who actually become pregnant and wish to teach into the ninth month, why couldn't the district cope with the uncertainty posed by pregnancy the same way it copes with other incapacities?

Finally, DeLaurier was a junior high school language teacher who had minimal responsibilities for supervising hallways and playgrounds. The testimony regarding increased girth and loss of agility was more appropriate to elementary school teachers, who must bend over small desks and supervise outdoor recreation. These concerns were not relevant to DeLaurier's particular job.

Retirement Age

In the 1970s there was increasing opposition to policies which imposed retirement on people simply because they had reached a certain age and which made no allowance for individual differences in the effects of aging. In many cases, these challenges led to upward revision of mandatory retirement ages. In some cases, mandatory retirement policies were eliminated. These changes came primarily as a result of actions by Congress and the state legislatures in response to the demands of senior-citizen groups.

Can a teacher be forced to retire at a certain age? Yes, but not before age 70. The U.S. Congress outlawed age discrimination against persons between the ages of 40 and 70 in the Age Discrimination in Employment Act amendments of 1978.[27] Elementary and secondary public school teachers may not be forced into retirement before the age of 70.[28] The previous age limit of 65 had been set by the Age Discrimination in Employment Act of 1967.

The new act closed a significant loophole. Courts had interpreted the earlier act as prohibiting the discharge of a worker because of age unless the worker were covered by a bona fide retirement insurance or pension program.[29] Thus, employers were permitted to retire workers covered by pension plans that allowed involuntary retirement before age 65. The 1978 Amendments specifically state that "no employee benefit plan shall require or permit the involuntary retirement of any individual . . . because of the age of such individual."[30]

A state legislature has the authority to set a mandatory retirement age for teachers which is consistent with the Age Discrimination Act.[31] The retirement age for teachers need not be the same as that for other public employees.[32] Local school districts may not adopt retirement policies that contravene or subvert the intentions of state legislatures.

Although there have been a few notable exceptions, the courts have been unsympathetic to public employees who have challenged mandatory retirement laws. Led by the U.S. Supreme Court, the courts have made it exceedingly difficult to challenge compulsory retirement on constitutional grounds.[33] The consensus of the courts is that the fixing of mandatory retirement ages for public employees is a matter for legislative determination.[34] Additional upward revisions in mandatory retirement ages will come in the legislatures, not in the courts.

Public employees have mounted legal challenges to compulsory retirement policies primarily on grounds that such policies deny them equal protection of the law. Why should a person be qualified to perform a job one year and not qualified the next? Why should a public employee be forced to retire at an earlier age than a comparable private employee?

The U.S. Supreme Court has rejected challenges based on denial of equal protection. The court has held that compulsory retirement of public employees is presumed to be constitutional. Therefore, those who would challenge such a policy must show that no legitimate state interest is served by the policy or that the particular policy is not rationally related to a legitimate state interest.

It is next to impossible to prove that any retirement policy is not rationally based.[35] As long as the facts on which any classification of employee is based could reasonably be thought true by the government decision maker, the policy is constitutional. Those who would challenge a policy must argue that the legislature had *no* reasonable basis for making the decision. Legislative determinations stand if the facts are arguable. Furthermore, the availability of other means to achieve the same legislative goals is irrelevant. It is the prerogative of legislators to choose from among competing alternative policies.

Local school district retirement policies also receive judicial deference. However local policies must be consistent with state and federal laws.[36] Teachers have successfully challenged local policies which forced earlier retirements than were specified in state laws. For example, in *Davis v. Griffin-Spaulding County Board of Education,* a Georgia school board forced a 68-year-old teacher to retire despite a state law that set 70 as the retirement age. The court awarded the teacher back pay and retirement fund contributions that would have been made had she been allowed to continue to teach.[37]

Furthermore, although court decisions on compulsory retirement suggest that *any* reason can justify such a policy, *some* reason must be established. *Gault v. Garrison* involved an Illinois teacher who was forced to retire at 65.[38] Illinois law does not force teachers to retire at any particular age; however, it did remove tenure protection at age 65.[39] School districts were permitted to contract with teachers over 65 on an annual basis or hire them as substitute teachers at much lower pay. The school board involved in the Gault challenge failed to present any evidence to justify its compulsory retirement policy. Thus, the court ruled that the policy was not justifiable. The court completely rejected the idea that the retirement policy protected the district against employees who were unfit to teach; normal dismissal procedures would accomplish this goal with greater assurance and fairness. Finally, the court noted that removing tenure protection from teachers at age 65 represented denial of equal protection. Without a justifiable and rational state purpose, the court could not sanction a total lack of procedural equality for teachers when they reach 65.

The Gault case stands out as an exception. When presented with reasons to justify the forced retirement of public employees, most courts have accepted the reasons and rejected equal-protection arguments. Thus, the issue of removal of tenure protection at a specific age is left hanging.

The purpose of tenure is to benefit the school system by providing stability of employment and protecting the school system from the ill effects of partisan or political manipulation. In considering school district retirement policies courts have accepted the desirability of a mix of older and younger teachers.[40] Newer and younger teachers are identified with educational innovation and flexibility. Thus, it is not unlikely that courts would accept a legislative conclusion that tenure protection should cease when teachers reach a certain age. Teachers would still be protected from age discrimination; however, school districts would be free to dismiss teachers for reasons other than cause, and teachers would bear the burden of proving age discrimination.

Violations of the Law

The law is a standard of acceptable behavior. For good or ill, teachers are examplars to their students. Teachers who fail to uphold the law or who flout the law are bad examples. Courts are understandably unsympathetic to them.

Criminal behavior, lawbreaking, and a pattern of contempt for law are *prima facie* evidence of unfitness to teach. They easily come within the meaning of the terms "justifiable cause" and "sufficient cause," found in numerous statutory lists of causes for teacher dismissal. In addition, some states specifically include illegal behavior as a cause for dismissal.[41] In California, North Carolina, Tennessee, and Texas, a conviction for a felony or for any crime involving moral turpitude is grounds for dismissal.

It is not necessary for a teacher to be *convicted* of a crime. A criminal act or advocacy of a criminal act can be sufficient basis for a charge of teacher unfitness. In *Board of Education v. Calderon,* a teacher was dismissed after he was arrested for homosexual acts.[42]

He was not convicted of the charge. The California Supreme Court decision in support of the dismissal centered on the differences between the standards required in criminal and civil actions. The court requires that guilt be proved *beyond a reasonable doubt* to sustain a criminal conviction; the school board requires only a *preponderance of evidence* to support dismissal.

By contrast, an Ohio court reversed the dismissal of a teacher who was convicted of a misdemeanor.

Hale v. Lancaster Board of Education[43]
Edward Hale was a new math teacher in the Lancaster, Ohio, school system. One evening he struck a parked car and left the scene of the accident without stopping or filing a report. Later, he was arrested, convicted of a misdemeanor, and sentenced to a fine of $50 and ten days in jail, suspended. Soon afterward, the school board gave him a hearing and terminated his contract.

Ohio says that a teacher's contract cannot be terminated except for gross inefficiency or immorality, for willful and persistent violations of rules, or for any other good and just cause.

The Ohio Supreme Court noted that the unnamed "other good and just cause" must be a fairly serious matter. Though Hale's behavior may have reflected adversely on his character and integrity, this single, isolated incident was not serious enough to represent just cause.

Use of Alcohol and Drugs

Education authorities express continuing concern about the effects of drugs and alcohol on students. The numerous state laws that require instruction in the harmful effects of drugs and alcohol attest to this concern.

Tenure laws also reflect this concern. In a number of states, abuse of drugs or alcohol is cited in the law as grounds for dismissal.[44] Some states incorporate such grounds under the umbrella of unfitness, incapacity, or incompetence; other statutes are more explicit. Texas, for example, includes "drunkenness" as a lawful cause for discharge. North Carolina cites "habitual or excessive use of alcohol or nonmedical use of a controlled substance."

Alcohol abuse and alcohol-inspired antisocial behavior have led to numerous dismissals. In *Bradford v. School District,* a South

Carolina teacher was fired for public drunkenness and for assaulting a police officer. A federal court ruled that South Carolina law gives school trustees the right to discharge teachers for good and sufficient reasons—and that the teacher's behavior met that criterion.[45] In *Hunter v. Board,* a Washington state teacher who had a history of alcohol abuse was fired after he pleaded guilty to driving while under the influence of intoxicating liquor. The Washington appeals court upheld his discharge for "excessive drinking."[46] A California court came to a similar conclusion:

Watson v. State Board of Education[47]

Joseph Watson, a California teacher, had been convicted of six alcohol-related offenses during the ten years preceding his application for a general secondary teaching certificate. When the certificate was denied, he sued.

The appeals court ruled that (1) Watson's use of alcohol was out of control and he was not a proper counselor to young people; (2) as a public drunk, Watson was a bad example of community standards; and (3) Watson's disregard for law was a bad example for students. The court said that Watson's behavior would give students a bad example of proper respect for law and authority. Thus, the denial of his teaching certificate was appropriate.

Governing Board v. Brennan[48]

Garnet E. Brennan, a Marin County teacher, filed an affidavit in support of a friend who was arrested and convicted for possession of marijuana. In her affidavit, Brennan said she used marijuana daily and knew it was not harmful.

On learning of the affidavit, her school board fired her. She sued for reinstatement.

The court ruled against her. It noted that she not only had admitted to an illegal act, she appeared to consider her illegal use of marijuana to be moral and proper. Furthermore, she had made the statement knowing that her views would be publicized.

Competent evidence on the probable negative effect of her conduct on student attitudes and behavior justified her dismissal.

Despite the evident bias against teachers who engage in this type of behavior, it is important to note that the teacher is entitled to all the protection of due process before dismissal. Furthermore, courts tend to require school boards to demonstrate the connection between the behavior and teaching responsibilities.

In *Lindgren v. Board,* a teacher was dismissed after he was arrested for driving without a license and for drunk driving (third offense). The Montana Supreme Court said:

> Dismissal of a teacher under contract requires a showing of immorality, unfitness, incompetence, or violation of the adopted policies of the trustees. The initial letter of dismissal failed to substantiate any causal relationship between appellant's violations and his performance of teaching duties. This court does not find, as a matter of law, that violations for driving under the influence of intoxicating liquor and driving without a valid driver's license are tantamount to "immorality, unfitness, incompetence, or violation of the adopted policies of such trustees."[49]

It seems likely that in preparing the initial dismissal letter, the trustees could have substantiated the causal relationships if they had understood the law.

Residency

Public employees have no right under the federal Constitution to live wherever they wish.[50] Fortunately, most school districts are content to let teachers live wherever they wish. Residency has been an issue primarily in large urban districts.

States and local governments, including school districts, may lawfully require employees to live within the boundaries of the employing government. Prior residency in the district cannot be made a condition of employment. However, a government may require employees to move into the district and to maintain residency while they hold their positions. Furthermore, a government may lawfully establish a residency requirement and require nonresident employees to establish residency by some reasonable future date.

In conclusion, the life-style revolution has come and gone, leaving new laws and court precedents that have clarified and expanded the teacher's zone of privacy. Teachers are now assured fair treatment in conflicts with school officials over their personal choices and protection from illegitimate encroachments on their privacy.

Notes to Chapter 8

1. See H. Gans, *The Levittowners* (New York: Random House, 1967); A. B. Hollingshead, *Elmstown's Youth* (New York: John Wiley and Sons, 1966); A. Vidich and L. Bensman, *Small Town in Massachusetts Society* (New York: Doubleday and Co., 1958); E.W. Anderson, *The Teacher's Contract and Other Legal Phases of Teacher Status* (New York: Teachers College, Columbia University, 1927). See also *Barth v. Hanna,* 158 Ill. App. 20 (1910), concerning a teacher who was slandered by a school board member.

2. See *Roe v. Wade,* 410 U.S. 113 (1973); *Eisenstadt v. Baird,* 405 U.S. 438 (1971); *Loving v. Virginia,* 388 U.S. (1966); *Griswold v. Connecticut,* 381 U.S. 479 (1965); *Meyer v. Nebraska,* 262 U.S. 390 (1922).

3. See *Shuman v. Philadelphia,* 470 F. Supp. 449 (E.D. Pa., 1979). Also see *Stoddard v. School District No. 1,* 429 F. Supp. 890, (D. Wyo., 1973), wherein the court said:

   > The right to be free from unwarranted governmental intrusions into one's privacy is a fundamental constitutional right . . . and such right of privacy embraces the right of an individual to attend church or not, to determine his or her own physical proportions, and to determine with whom he or she will associate.

   One element of protection is the right to sue for violation of the constitutional right to privacy; see *Board of Trustees v. Holso,* 584 P. 2d 1009 (Supreme Ct. of Wyo., 1978). David Holso, an unmarried teacher, was engaged in a relationship with an unmarried female teacher. A trial judge found that the board acted "knowingly, intentionally, and maliciously" in its discharge of Holso for immorality. The Wyoming Supreme Court ruled that the superintendent, having been maliciously motivated, was personally liable for violating Holso's right of privacy.

4. *Kelly v. Johnson,* 425 U.S. 238 (1976).

5. *Miller v. School District,* 495 F. 2d 658 (7th Cir., 1974).

6. *Tardif v. Quinn,* 545 F. 2d 761 (1st Cir., 1976).

7. *East Hartford Education Association v. School District,* 562 F. 2d 838 (2nd. Cir., 1977). See also *Blanchet v. Vermillion Parish School Board,* 220 S. 2d 534 (La. App., 1969).

8. *Rawlings v. Butler,* 290 S.W. 2d 801 (Ky. App., 1956). See also "Wearing of Religious Garb by Public School Teachers," in *American Law Report* 2d, vol. 60 (Rochester, N.Y.: Lawyers Cooperative Publishing Co.), p. 360.

9. *Moore v. Board of Education,* 212 N.E. 2d 833 (Ohio Ct. of Common Pleas, 1965).

10. *Arkansas Statutes,* Sec. 80-1261 (Supp., 1979).

11. *Oregon Revised Statutes,* Sec. 342.650 (1973 replacement part); *North Dakota Century Code,* Sec. 15-47-29, 30 (replacement vol. 3, 1971).

12. *Braxton v. Board,* 303 F. Supp. 958 (M.D. Fla., 1969); contrast with *Miller v. School District* (1974). See also *Conrad v. Goolsby,* 350 F. Supp. 713 (D.C. Miss., 1972), and *Rider v. Pawnee* (reported in *United States Law Week,* May 25, 1973), wherein the court ruled that a school's hair-length regulation did not

infringe on Indian students' freedom of speech or exercise of religion.

13. *Finot v. Pasadena City Board of Education,* 58 Cal. Rptr. 520 (App., 1967).

14. *Parolisi v. Board of Examiners,* 285 N.Y.S. 2d 936 (Supreme Ct., 1967).

15. *Blodgett v. Board of Trustees, Tamalpais,* 97 Cal. Rptr. 406 (App., 1971).

16. *Erb v. Iowa State Board of Public Instruction,* 216 N.W. 2d 339 (Supreme Ct. of Iowa, 1974).

17. *Reinhardt v. Board of Education,* 311 N.E. 2d 710 (Ill. App., 1974); vacated, 329 N.E. 2d 218 (Supreme Ct. of Ill., 1975).

18. *Fisher v. Snyder,* 346 F. Supp. 396 (D. Neb., 1972); sustained, 476 F. 2d 375 (8th Cir.,, 1973).

19. *Sullivan v. Meade Independent School District,* 387 F. Supp. 1237 (D. S.D., 1975). See also *Brown v. Bathke,* 416 F. Supp. 1194 (D. Neb., 1976); *Hollenbaugh v. Carnegie Free Library,* 436 F. Supp. 1328 (W.D. Pa., 1977).

20. *Acanfora v. Montgomery Board of Education,* 359 F. Supp. 843 (D. Md., 1973). In *Goldin v. Board,* 364 N.Y.S. 2d 440 (1974), a majority of the New York Court of Appeals identified two circumstances that would limit the right to privacy:

> In our view what might otherwise be considered private conduct beyond the scope of licit concern of school officials ceases to be such in at least either of two circumstances—if the conduct directly affects the performance of the professional responsibilities of the teacher *or if,* without contribution on the part of the school officials, the conduct has become the subject of such public notoriety as significantly and reasonably to impair the capability of the particular teacher to discharge the responsibilities of his position.

Also see *Boyette v. State Professional Practices Council,* 346 So. 2d 598 (Fla. App., 1977).

In *Gish v. Board,* 366 A. 2d 1337 (N.J. Super., 1976), the court upheld a school board's request that a teacher who was a homosexual activist submit to a psychiatric examination. The court said there had not been a single instance of undue classroom conduct or action on the part of the teacher with respect to students. Nevertheless, the board's belief, with supportive corroboration from two psychiatrists, that the teacher's actions displayed "evidence of deviation from normal mental health which may affect his ability to teach, discipline, and associate with the students" was sufficient justification for this demand. Thus, the court appears to have ruled that informed speculation that a teacher's performance may be affected was sufficient justification in the absence of any evidence. Although a psychiatric examination is a significant intrusion, it is worth noting that the court was not sustaining a transfer or dismissal.

21. *Gaylord v. Tacoma School District No. 10,* 559 P. 2d 1340 (Supreme Ct. of Wash., 1977). In *Burton v. Cascade School District,* 353 F. Supp. 254 (D.C. Ore., 1973); affirmed, 512 F. 2d 850 (9th Cir.); cert. denied, 423 U.S. 839, a federal district court reversed a school board's dismissal of a homosexual teacher for immorality. The Oregon immorality statute, which is similar to Washington's, was declared unconstitutionally vague. In this case, the

untenured teacher was awarded compensatory damages for the duration of her contract but was not reinstated. Thus, even though her cause had been vindicated, she was out of a job. From the perspectives of both school boards, the Gaylord and Burton cases achieved similar results.

22. Anderson, *Teacher's Contract*, p. 69.

23. Ibid., p. 118.

24. *People ex. rel. Templeton et al. v. Board*, 102 N.E. 2d 751 (Ill. App., 1952); *People ex. rel. Christner v. Hamilton*, 59 N.E. 2d 198 (Ill. App., 1945).

25. *Cleveland Board of Education v. LaFleur*, 414 U.S. 632 (1974).

26. *DeLaurier v. San Diego Unified School District*, 588 F. 2d 674 (9th Cir., 1976).

27. Public Law 92-256, passed by the 95th Congress on April 6, 1978, amended the Age Discrimination in Employment Act of 1967, 29 USCS, Section 621 et seq.

28. Section 3 of the 1978 amendments specifically excludes tenured college faculty age 65 and older until July 1982. The 1967 act had permitted employers to use age as a basis for classifying workers "where age is a bona fide occupational qualification reasonably necessary to the normal operation of the particular business." An employer would have to show reason to believe that all persons in a certain age group would be unable to perform the job or that it would be impractical to deal with persons in the group on an individualized basis. See *Arritt v. Gisell* 567 F. 2d 1267 (4th Cir., 1977). It is difficult to see how this exception could be applied to teachers.

29. *Zinger v. Blanchette*, 549 F. 2nd 901 (3rd Cir., 1977); cert. denied, 434 U.S. 1008. See also *United Airlines Inc. v. McMann*, 434 U.S. 192, 218 (1977), and Justice Marshall's dissenting opinion.

30. Public Law 92-256, Sec. 2(a).

31. *Usury v. Board of Education*, 421 F. Supp. 718 (D.C. Utah, 1976); *Kuhar v. Greensburg-Salem School District*, 466 F. Supp. 806 (W.D. Pa., 1979). State legislatures have already begun to bring their statutes into conformity. In Indiana, the legislature raised from 66 to 71 the age at which members of the retirement fund agree to give up their eligibility to continue to teach; see *Indiana Statutes Annotated*, Sec. 21-6, 1-5-6 (Cum. Supp., 1979). In Illinois (P.A. 81, 1979), the legislature raised the mandatory retirement age of Chicago teachers from 65 to 70. See also *New Jersey Statutes Annotated*, Sec. 18A, 16-43 (Cum. Supp., 1979).

32. *Trafelet v. Thompson*, 594 F. 2d 623 (7th Cir., 1979); *Fulton County School District v. Sanders*, 248 S.E. 3d 670 (Supreme Ct. of Ga., 1978).

33. *Massachusetts Board of Retirement v. Murgia*, 427 U.S. 307 (1976); *Vance v. Bradley*, 474 F. Supp. 882 (W.D. Wis., 1979); *Slate v. Noll*, 474 F. Supp. 882 (W.D. Wis., 1979).

34. *Fazekas v. University of Houston*, 565 S.W. 2d 299 (Texas Ct. of Civil Appeals, 1978); *O'Neil v. Baine*, 568 S.W. 2d 761 (Supreme Ct. of Mo., 1978).

35. *Slate v. Noll* at 886; *Fulton v. Sanders*.

36. Courts consistently look to state legislatures to take the lead in identifying mandatory retirement ages. See *DeShon v. Bettendorf Community School*

District, 284 N.W. 2d 329, 332 (Supreme Ct. of Iowa, 1979); *University of South Carolina v. Bateson,* 246 S.E. 2d 882 (Supreme Ct. of S.C., 1978).

37. *Davis v. Griffin-Spaulding County Board of Education,* 445 F. Supp. 1048 (N.D. Ga., 1975).

38. *Gault v. Garrison,* 569 F. 2d 993 (7th Cir., 1977).

39. *Illinois Revised Annotated Statutes,* Ch. 122, Sec. 24-11; *Kennedy v. Community School District,* 319 N.E. 2d 243 (Ill. App., 1974). Illinois is not alone in withdrawing tenure from teachers who reach a specified age. See *Belcher v. Gish,* 555 S.W. 2d 264 (Supreme Ct. of Ky., 1977); *Lewis v. Tucson School District No. 1,* 531 P. 2d 199 (Ariz. App., 1975); *Monier v. Todd County School District,* 245 N.W. 2d 503 (Supreme Ct. of S.D., 1976).

40. *Palmer v. Ticcione,* 576 F. 2d 459, 462 (2nd Cir., 1978); *DeShon v. Bettendorf* at 333, *Kuhar v. Greensburg-Salem* at 814; *King v. Board,* 555 S.W. 2d 925 (Texas Ct. of Civil Appeals, 1977).

41. *California Education Code Annotated,* Sec. 44345; *North Carolina General Statutes,* Sec. 115-142 (1979 Supp.); *Tennessee Code Annotated,* Sec. 49-1401(b); *Texas Statutes Annotated* (Vernon's), Sec. 13.109(2); *Georgia Code Annotated,* Sec. 32-2101C (a)(s). Also see *Ore. Rev. Stat.,* Sec. 342.865(f); *N.D. Cent. Code,* Sec. 15-47-38; *South Carolina Code,* Sec. 59-25-430.

42. *Board of Education v. Calderon,* 110 Cal. Rptr. 916 (Supreme Ct., 1973); cert. denied, 419 U.S. 807 (1974). See also *Jenkyns v. Board,* 294 F. 2d 266 (C.P. D.C., 1961).

43. *Hale v. Lancaster Board of Education,* 234 N.E. 2d 583 (Supreme Ct. of Ohio, 1968).

44. *Texas Statutes Annotated,* Sec. 13.109(3); *N.C. Gen. Stat.,* Sec. 115-142 F (1979 Supp.). See also *Tenn. Code Ann.,* Sec. 49-1401(e); *Calif. Educ. Code Ann.,* Sec. 44345.

45. *Bradford v. School District,* 364 F. 2d 185 (4th Cir., 1966).

46. *Hunter v. Board,* 536 P. 2d 1209 (Wash. App., 1975).

47. *Watson v. State Board of Education,* 99 Cal. Rptr. 712 (App., 1971).

48. *Governing Board v. Brennan,* 95 Cal. Rptr. 712 (App., 1971).

49. *Lindgren v. Board,* 558 P. 2d 468 (Supreme Ct. of Mont., 1976).

50. *McCarthy v. Philadelphia Civil Service Commission,* 424 U.S. 645 (1976); *Cook County College Teachers Union, Local 1600 v. Taylor,* 432 F. Supp. 270 (N.D. Ill., 1977); *Abrahams v. Civil Service Commission,* 319 A. 2d 483 (Supreme Ct. of N.J., 1974). Whereas some states have passed laws prohibiting local districts from imposing residency requirements, other states permit residency requirements. California *(Educ. Code Ann.,* Sec. 44849) prohibits residency requirements. Illinois recently outlawed residency requirements for all districts except Chicago (Public Act 81-151, 1979). Maine permits local district ordinances and collective-bargaining agreements which require new employees to be residents; see *Maine Revised Statutes Annotated,* Vol. 2, Title 20, Sec. 863: Residency (1979 Supp.). See also *Johnson v. Dixon,* 501 S.W. 2d 256 (Supreme Ct. of Ky.), which reversed a school board that sought to give job preferences to natives of the county.

RELATED RESOURCES
in the ERIC System

The resources described in this section have been entered into the ERIC (Educational Resources Information Center) system. Each is identified by a six-digit number and two letters: "EJ" for journal articles, "ED" for other documents.

If you want to read a document with an ED number, check to see whether your local library or instructional media center subscribe to the ERIC microfiche collection. (For a list of libraries in your area that subscribe to the ERIC system, write to ERIC/ChESS, 855 Broadway, Boulder, Colorado 80302.)

If an ERIC collection is not accessible, or if you want a personal copy of the document in either microfiche (MF) or paper copy (PC), write to ERIC Document Reproduction Services (EDRS), Computer Microfilm International Corporation, P.O. Box 190, Arlington, Virginia. All orders must be accompanied by payment in full, including prepaid postage. Prices (correct as of September 1, 1980) are cited for each ED document. (Note that for some documents paper copies are either not available or must be ordered from the publisher or distributor instead of from EDRS.)

If your local library does not have a journal article that you want, you may write for one or more reprints to University Microfilms, 300 North Zeeb Road, Ann Arbor, Michigan 48106. The following information is needed: title of periodical or journal, title of article, author's name, date of issue, volume number, issue number, and page numbers. All orders must be accompanied by payment in full, plus postage.

General

Bright, Myron H. "The Constitution, the Judges, and the School Administrator." *NASSP Bulletin* 63, no. 424 (February 1979), pp. 74-83. EJ 196 061.

Reviews U.S. Supreme Court and federal appellate court decisions re students' and teachers' rights, particularly due-process rights.

Drake, Jackson M. *Landmark Court Cases Affecting School Governance,* vol. 2. Tempe, Ariz.: Arizona State University, Bureau of Educational Research and Services, 1979. EDRS price: MF $0.83, PC $4.82; plus postage (68 pp.). ED 168 192.

Reviews landmark decisions of the U.S. Supreme Court on various kinds of school issues.

Fischer, Louis. "The Civil Rights of Teachers in Post-Industrial Society." *High School Journal* 61, no. 8 (May 1978), pp. 380-392. EJ 184 431.

Sketches the major recent developments in the civil rights of teachers.

Loewenthal, Alfred, and Robert Nielsen. *Bargaining for Academic Democracy.* Washington, D.C.: American Federation of Teachers, 1976. EDRS price: MF $0.83, PC $1.82; plus postage (11 pp.). Also available from AFT, 11 Dupont Circle, N.W., Washington, DC 20036 (item no. 618; $0.25 per copy, $20.00 per 100). ED 169 817.

Discusses academic collective bargaining and its historical foundations, primarily at the university level.

McGhehey, M.A., ed. *School Law Update—1977.* Topeka: National Organization on Legal Problems in Education, 1978. EDRS price: MF $0.83; plus postage (371 pp.). Paper copy not available from EDRS; order from NOLPE, 5401 S.W. Seventh Ave., Topeka, KS 66606 ($9.95). ED 169 635.

A collection of 26 addresses on issues related to school law at all levels, presented at NOLPE's 23rd annual convention.

Stern, Ralph D., ed. *The School Principal and the Law.* Topeka: National Organization on Legal Problems of Education, 1978. Not available from EDRS; order from NOLPE, 5401 S.W. Seventh Ave., Topeka, KS 66606 (252 pp.; $11.95). ED 172 327.

A collection of 12 papers by experts in school law and administration dealing with the role of the public school principal and its legal implications.

Zirkel, Perry A., and Robert J. Martin. "School Boards Are Scoring More Victories in the Supreme Court Than You Might Think." *American School Board Journal* 165, no. 12 (December 1978), pp. 43-44. EJ 192 408.

Points out that school boards have achieved the most success in court cases involving student and teacher rights and responsibilities.

Job Protection

Ames, Peter J. "When Tenure Contracts Can't Be Honored." *AGB Reports* 20, no. 6 (November/December 1978), pp. 33-40. EJ 194 373.

Describes a procedure for determining priorities for the termination of experienced teachers which is based on the principle of "relatively less merit"; a rebuttal is included.

"Iowa Public School Teachers: Procedural Due Process Requirements for Contract Termination." *Drake Law Review* 28, no. 1 (1978/79), pp. 121-145. EJ 207 991.

Examines the procedural due-process rights of teachers in Iowa.

Van Dyke, H.C., and R.N. Arkell. "Human Rights Legislation and the Employment of Teachers." *Education Canada* 18, no. 2 (Summer 1978), pp. 44-47. EJ 188 168.

Looks at teacher employment procedures in terms of what practices might be considered discriminatory.

Yates, Michael D. "Public School Teachers' Unions and Management Rights in Pennsylvania." *Journal of Collective Negotiations in the Public Sector* 7, no. 1 (1978), pp. 61-72. EJ 186 755.

Analyzes contracts from various state school districts in terms of management control, fiscal problems, and supply of teachers.

Professional Rights and Responsibilities

Miller, Pamela C. "Copyright: When Is Fair Use Not Fair?" *Educational Technology* 19, no. 1 (January 1979), pp. 44-47. EJ 203 464.

Reviews section 107 of the Copyright Act of 1976 and discusses the concept of fair use in terms of its implications for teachers and students.

Ochoa, Anna S. "Censorship: Does Anybody Care?" *Social Education* 43, no. 4 (April 1979), pp. 304-309. EJ 198 695.

Focuses on the nature and extent of censorship in social studies materials and instruction in the United States and suggests ways in which teachers and professional organizations can and should deal with this issue.

Scott, William C. "A Middle-School's Plan for an After-School Detention Program." *NASSP Bulletin* 63, no. 424 (February 1979), pp. 55-58. EJ 196 057.

Describes a detention program that emphasizes positive learning rather than punishment.

Swan, Malcolm D. *Outdoor Education: Community Studies Through Field Experiences.* University Park, N.M.: ERIC Clearinghouse on Rural Education and Small Schools, New Mexico State University, 1979. EDRS price: MF $0.83, PC $4.82; plus postage (72 pp.). Also available from National Educational Laboratory Publishers, Inc., 813 Airport Blvd., Austin, TX 78702 (EC-074; $6.50). ED 167 317.

Offers guidelines for planning field trips with students, including an explanation of legal responsibilities and safety precautions.

Valente, William D. "Overview of Constitutional Developments Affecting Individual and Parental Liberty Interests in Elementary and Secondary Education." Paper prepared from an address delivered to the Lawyers' Clinic on Parental Liberty in Education, Washington, D.C., December 1978. EDRS price: MF $0.83, PC $3.32; plus postage (39 pp.). ED 168 174.

Reviews judicial and constitutional interpretations of parents' options in making educational decisions for their children and attempting to influence public school programs.

Personal Rights and Freedoms

Bayes, Bonnie, and Patricia Lines, eds. *The People Power Papers: A New Birth of Freedom.* Seattle: People Power Coalition, 1977. EDRS price: MF $0.83; plus postage (143 pp.). Paper copy not available.

Includes a section on freedom in public education which discusses the civil rights of students and teachers.

Flygare, Thomas J. "The Free Speech Rights of Teachers: Public v. Private Expression." *Phi Delta Kappan* 60, no. 3 (November 1978), pp. 242-43. EJ 190 458.

Discusses the Givhan case, in which a teacher was dismissed for private rather than public speech.

Honig, Doug. "Gay Teachers and the Right to Teach." *Educentric* 42 (Spring 78), pp. 13-14. EJ 183 646.

Describes a case in the state of Washington in which a teacher was dismissed for "immorality" after he acknowledged his homosexuality.

Middleton, Richard T. "A Recent Mississippi Court Decision Affects Education and Women's Rights." *Negro Educational Review* 30, no. 1 (January 1979), pp. 47-52. EJ 197 340.

Discusses the implication for women's rights of the decision to employ school teachers even though they are unwed mothers.

O'Reilly, Robert C. "A Personnel Administration Problem for Schools: Equality, Pregnancy and Disability." Paper presented at a meeting of the National Conference of Professors of Education Administration, Edmonton, Alberta, Canada, August 1979. EDRS price: MF $0.83, PC $1.82; plus postage (21 pp.). ED 173 945.

Explains Public Law 95-555, which prohibits discrimination in employment on the basis of pregnancy, childbirth, or related medical conditions.

Phay, Robert E. "Dress Codes for Teachers." *School Law Bulletin* 10, no. 1 (January 1979), pp. 1, 11-12. EJ 196 120.

Reviews recent court decision upholding the right of school boards to set "reasonable" standards for teachers' dress and hair styles.

Sinowitz, Betty E. "The Teacher and the Law: Association Activity Rights." *Today's Education* 67, no. 2 (April/May 1978), pp. 20-21. EJ 186 144.

Explains constitutional and statutory remedies for protecting teachers' right to communicate and associate with one another in teacher organizations.